THE ART OF
ARCHITECTURAL
ILLUSTRATION

First published in the United States of America and Canada by:
McGraw Hill

All other distribution:
Rockport Publishers
Rockport, Massachusetts

ISBN 0-07-024765-X

10 9 8 7 6 5 4 3 2 1

Designer: Laura Herrmann Design
Cover Design: Margaret Webster-Shapiro/Kathleen Kelley
Cover Images: James C. Smith
Back Jacket Images: Left to right, Lee Dunnette, Willem van den Hoed

Manufactured in Hong Kong by Regent Publishing Services Limited

THE ART OF ARCHITECTURAL ILLUSTRATION

Edited by Gordon Grice

McGraw-Hill
New York • Washington D.C. • San Francisco • Montreal • Toronto

ACKNOWLEDGEMENTS

The editor wishes to thank the following people for their assistance
and/or support during the compilation of this book:

Tamotsu Yamamoto, Boston, ASAP President and Japanese consultant
Steve Oles, Newton, Mass., and Frank Costantino, Winthrop, Mass., ASAP co-founders

Arthur Furst, Norfolk, Mass., editor extraordinaire at Rockport
Rob Perlman, Natick, Mass., founder of Resource World
Tom Schaller, New York
Fanny Ghorayeb, Toronto

PROJECT
Mnemotec Shelter
Vittorio, Abruzzi, Italy

ARCHITECT
Maragna Arcitect Inc.

ILLUSTRATOR
Gordon Grice

RENDERING SIZE
18" x 26" (46 cm x 66 cm)

MEDIUM
Ink and pencil crayon on mylar

Table of Contents

PROJECT
San Francisco Museum of Modern Art
San Francisco, California

ARCHITECT
Mario Botta

ILLUSTRATOR
Frank M. Costantino

RENDERING SIZE
8" x 10" (20 cm x 25 cm)

MEDIUM
Watercolor for Premier Edition note card series

Introduction

By Gordon Grice

Projects usually begin with a phone call. Callers identify themselves and, if they are unknown to me, the names of their companies and the cities from which they are calling. Then, typically, the questions begin:

"Are you still doing renderings?" I am asked this question frequently; maybe I should take the hint.

"How is your time, over the next...?"

"Would you be interested in having a look at...?"

"How much would it cost to...?"

"How long would it take to...?"

"Can you start right away?"

The business of architectural rendering, it seems, is answering questions. When the talking is done, the drawings have their turn:

"What will the scheme look like?"

"How will it integrate with its enviroment?"

"Will the clients/investors/purchasers/neighbors/ planners...like it?"

But the subject of architectural illustration raises questions of a much deeper nature that are too infrequently asked, and not easily answered.

What is the purpose of rendering?

Is it a fine art, or is it commercial, technical, editorial, visionary, or something else entirely?

Is it an art at all or is an imitative reduction of architecture?

Is it useful? Is it relevant? Is it all of these things or none of them?

We hope that the work represented in this book, even as it pleases and possibly astounds you, will help lead you to answers to some of these more perplexing questions.

• • •

For a more detailed response to questions concerning architectural illustration that you may or may not have thought to ask, our four essayists offer their own views, personal and general, on a range of topics. At the very least, these written pieces should provide new ways of looking at the work of architectural illustrators.

One subject that is of universal interest to commercial illustrators is examined by Frank Costantino: the delicate balance between objectivity and subjectivity. Commercial illustration always has an aim: a subject to be described, a point to be made, a particular discovery to be revealed; but fine art must transcend its subject matter. The success of Frank's ruminations on the aesthetic potential of his own drawings, as with our other contributions, is evident in the work.

In Gilbert Gorski's essay, the matter of tool selection is explored in a new light. With regard to architectural illustration, how does the selection of drawing instruments affect the nature of drawing, and more critically, the very nature of the architecture that it seeks to portray? In a well-reasoned argument, Gilbert suggests that the effect of drawing styles and instruments on architectural expression is firmly established. You may already have suspected that computer technology has begun to alter the built environment, but it has done so in ways you may not have considered.

From a more personal point of view, Andy Hickes provides a reluctant testimonial to the use of computers in the studio. In Andy's own work, and in the work of most illustrators in this book, computers have played a significant role. Some illustrators (Andy among them) use the computer as a painting tool to execute finished art, others as a 3-D modeling tool with which they render electronically or manually. Still others employ digital technology's unique characteristics to construct theoretical views, time lapses, and animations. The goal of an artist is to make technique transparent: *Ars est celare artem.* Within the pages of this book, the contribution of computers is ubiquitous, but, I'll wager, almost invisible.

A particularly important facet of architectural illustration is addressed by Tom Schaller in his piece, "A Building is not a Drawing." This seemingly obvious title refers to a misapprehension shared by many illustrators, architects, and critics: that the creative impetus for architectural illustration is the same as that for architectural design, only expressed in a different and, possibly, less-complete way. Tom's persuasive exposition points out the unlikeliness of this view, and the need to abandon it, if an understanding of architectural illustration is to be realized.

To my mind, Tom's discussion leads up to a slightly more insidious misconception: that the primary goal and noblest aspiration of any architectural illustration is to further the development of a particular piece of architecture. A well-known quotation by Hugh Ferriss, one of North America's pre-eminent architect/illustrators seems to support this:

> Architectural rendering is the means to an end and that end is architecture.

These words have become a virtual credo for professional renderers. They help to place the block of rendering neatly into the wall of architecture, and lend much comfort to renderers and architects alike. I, for one, agree with the statement, but not at all with the limited definition of "architecture" that many architects infer but that Ferriss probably never intended. This limited definition is made more apparent in the following quotation, in which Jean Ferriss Leich quotes her father in *Architectural Record, 1956:*

> Rendering should be regarded merely as a means "to help get projects designed; to help get the designs understood by all concerned; and thereby to help get buildings built."

and then there is Henry Cobb's definition, written in the foreword to *Architecture in Perspective 10:*

> They [perspectivists] are the servants of servants...

As helpful as these explanations appear to be, they are in fact quite misleading. For example, many of Ferriss's own drawings, and particularly those for which he is most renowned, are the end products of architectural investigation, not the means to a specific end. His drawings have certainly assisted in the design, presentation, and construction of many buildings, but frequently, specific drawings were not intended to further the cause of specific buildings. If anything, Ferriss's drawings more effectively convince us of the power of drawing to help change our ideas about the environment, than of the power of buildings to actually accomplish those changes.

Architecture exists because we need buildings, but if every architectural idea could only ever be evaluated by building it, our world would contain a lot more unpleasant and inadequate structures than it currently does. Architecture is really a realm of ideas, and many of those ideas can be more eloquently expressed in forms other than built structures. Building may be the most important, but it is not the only legitimate result of an architectural exercise. Architectural illustration offers some convincing evidence of this.

• • •

In the following pages, we present the work of thirty-five talented commercial renderers, whose work ranges across a wide spectrum of contemporary technique, approach, and subject matter. The illustrators have one thing in common: driven by a desire for obscurity, sleeplessness, and underwhelming financial gain, they have abandoned or nearly abandoned all other means of support in order to earn their living in a rare profession. In this world of some five billion people, perhaps five thousand are commercial renderers. They are one in a million. In the following pages, you will see the product of a further distillation: from five thousand to thirty-five, among the best to be found in the world today. We present this work for your enjoyment and edification, but don't be afraid to ask more questions.

AZ Project Inc.
563 Ishiyama, Minamiku,
Sapporo 005 Japan
011-591-1683
011-591-9519 fax

Sachiko Asai

Sachiko Asai was born in Obihiro, Hokkaido, Japan, in 1953 and began to study perspective in 1971. In 1984 she established AZ Project of perspective, an environmentally conscious company in which a sculptor and professional perspectivist can have a conversation with the globe. AZ Project attempts to represent a message from the globe by its illustrations and formative arts.

In 1992, the AZ gallery "Sun Dial" was opened. Since then, Asai's original works have been permanently shown in the gallery, and have also appeared in Architectural Rendering No. 1, New Office Design (1990), Architectural Rendering No. 2, Leisure & Resort Space (1990), Architectural Rendering No. 3, Waterfronts (1991), Architectural Illustrations parts II and III (1992) and Details in Architectural Rendering (1994).

Asai's works "Beat from the Sea Bottom" and "DNA of Dune" participated in the Environment Art Great Award '93. The latter received a prize of excellent work. "Beat from the Sea Bottom" is a designed picture of the symbolic green zone to be rendered in the gateway to Kansai International Airport.

The "DNA of Dune" is a part of an image depicting several pedestrian bridges and rest spots along the sand hill area of the Sea of Japan coast.

PROJECT
The Center of
Forest Products

ARCHITECTS
& CLIENT
Sachiko Asai

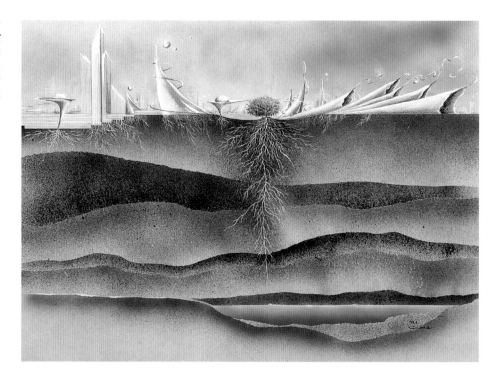

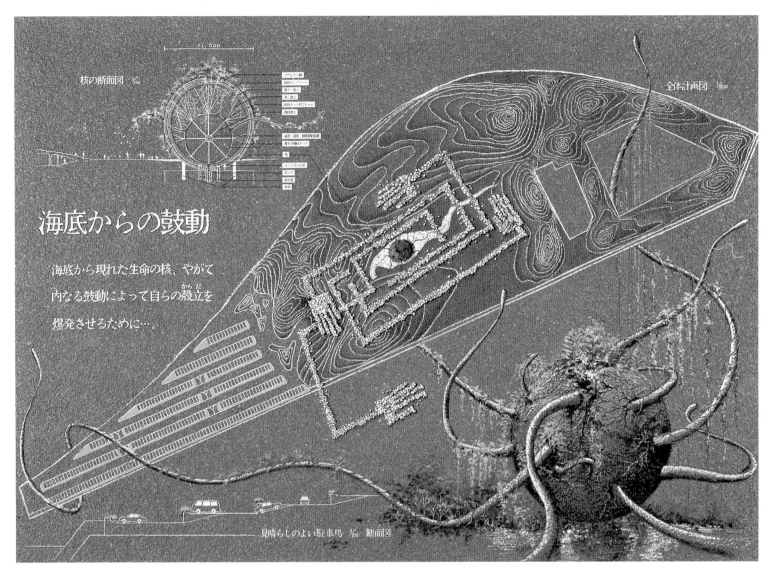

海底からの鼓動

海底から現れた生命の核、やがて
内なる鼓動によって自らの殻立を
爆発させるために…。

PROJECT
Beat from the Sea Bottom, No. 1
ARCHITECTS & CLIENT
Kenichi Asai

海底からの鼓動

PROJECT
Beat from the Sea Bottom
ARCHITECTS & CLIENT
Kenichi Asai

Sachiko Asai   **11**

砂丘の記憶
SAKYU NO KIOKU

遠い記憶の中で、生きつづけている命の戦は
いつか砂になる時を待つ岩かもしれない。
綿々と満ち引きを繰りかえす海の際で、
無数の粒となり陸と海とをつなぐもの…。

記憶は語りつがれながら形を変えいつかこなごなになり歴史という箱にしまわれる。

PROJECT
The DNA of Dune
ARCHITECTS & CLIENT
Kenichi Asai

PROJECT
Eve
ARCHITECTS & CLIENT
Sachiko Asai

PROJECT
Junior high school in Iwamizawa
CLIENT
Atelier aku Co.

PROJECT
Project in Jozankei, Japan
CLIENT
Atelier aku Co.

PROJECT
Seaside project in Otaru, Japan
ARCHITECTS & CLIENT
Kenichi Asai

PROJECT
Farming village park in Niki, Japan
ARCHITECTS & CLIENT
Sachiko Asai

PROJECT
Farming village park in Iwamizawa, Japan
ARCHITECTS & CLIENT
Sachiko Asai

PROJECT
An easy-going father
ARCHITECTS & CLIENT
Sachiko Asai

PROJECT
Robotto House

ARCHITECTS & CLIENT
Sachiko Asai

305 NORTHERN BOULEVARD
GREAT NECK, NEW YORK 11021
516-466-0470

PROJECT
345 Hudson Street
New York, New York
Rehabilitation of Building Entrance

CLIENT
Berg & Forster

RENDERING SIZE
19" x 15.5" (48 cm x 39 cm)

MEDIUM
Tempera

Richard C. Baehr, A.I.A.

Richard Baehr is an architect who specializes in architectural rendering, specifically tempera. Having worked professionally in pencil, pen and ink, watercolor, charcoal pencil, and markers, he has found that tempera is a medium versatile and powerful enough to express virtually any architectural or design idea. A photorealistic technique, tempera has the added advantage of allowing changes when necessary.

Baehr works with local clients, as well as regional, national, and international architects, owners, and developers. In one instance, plans for a Berlin office building were faxed from Germany, and the finished rendering was shipped via FedEx, the effort taking no longer than a local project.

Baehr has exhibited in the United States, Canada, Europe, and Asia, and has lectured in New York, Boston, Toronto, and Osaka. He is a graduate of the Cooper Union School of Architecture and the University of Cincinnati School of Applied Arts. He is a member of the American Institute of Architects, the American Society of Architectural Perspectivists, and the New York Society of Renderers. His book *Architectural Rendering in Tempera* was published in 1995 by Van Nostrand Reinhold.

PROJECT
Port Washington
Library Addition
Port Washington, New York

CLIENT
Gwathmey Siegel & Assoc.

RENDERING SIZE
33" x 175" (38 cm x 84 cm)

MEDIUM
Tempera

PROJECT
Trump Palace
New York, New York

OWNER/DEVELOPER
Donald J. Trump

CLIENT
Frank Williams & Associates

RENDERING SIZE
18" x 37.5" (46 cm x 92 cm)

MEDIUM
Tempera

PROJECT
Lobby, 599 Lexington Avenue
New York, New York

CLIENT
Edward Larrabee Barnes-John M.Y. Lee

RENDERING SIZE
20.5" x 20.5" (52 cm x 52 cm)

MEDIUM
Tempera

PROJECT
Long Island Office Building
New York, New York

CLIENT
Mojo Stumer

RENDERING SIZE
33" x 17" (84 cm x 43 cm)

MEDIUM
Tempera

PROJECT
Atrium Lobby, International Place
Boston, Massachusetts

CLIENT
Johnson & Burgee

RENDERING SIZE
33" x 19" (84 cm x 48 cm)

MEDIUM
Tempera

PROJECT
Terminal Interior
Baltimore Washington International Airport
Baltimore, Maryland
CLIENT
William Nicholas Bodouva & Associates
RENDERING SIZE
34" x 16" (86 cm x 41 cm)
MEDIUM
Tempera

PROJECT
Trump International Hotel and Tower
New York, New York
CLIENT
Philip Johnson, Ritchie & Fiore
RENDERING SIZE
23" x 11.5" (58 cm x 29 cm)
MEDIUM
Tempera

BAEHR '92

PROJECT
U.S. Courthouse, Foley Square
New York, New York

CLIENT
Kohn Pedersen Fox

RENDERING SIZE
20.5" x 30"   (52 cm x 76 cm)

MEDIUM
Tempera

PROJECT
Photo Montage, International Place
Boston, Massachusetts

CLIENT
Johnson & Burgee

RENDERING SIZE
40" x 21.5" (102 cm x 55 cm)

MEDIUM
Tempera

PROJECT
Photo Montage, World Financial Center
New York, New York

CLIENT
Cesar Pelli & Associates

RENDERING SIZE
47" x 20" (119 cm x 51 cm)

MEDIUM
Tempera

PROJECT
Trump International Hotel and Tower
New York, New York

CLIENT
Philip Johnson, Ritchie & Fiore

RENDERING SIZE
16" x 33" (41 cm x 84 cm)

MEDIUM
Tempera

COMMERCIAL ARTISTRY
1009 PARK AVENUE
MOODY, ALABAMA 35004

PROJECT
Riverside Refractories Inc.
Pell City, Alabama, Private Collection
RENDERING SIZE
17" x 25" (43 cm x 64 cm)
MEDIUM
Gouache

PROJECT
Blast Furnace, Private Collection
RENDERING SIZE
17" x 22" (43 cm x 56 cm)
MEDIUM
Marker

Anita S. Bice

Anita Bice is a versatile artist who strives to attain a high level of excellence with all subject matter and media. As a 1981 graduate of Samford University, Birmingham, Alabama, in Fine Art and Business, she continued her training and received a degree in Architectural Illustration from the American Academy of Art in Chicago, Illinois, in 1984. Since that time, she has worked primarily as an architectural illustrator in the southeastern region of the United States. Bice's clients include architects, developers, interior designers, engineering firms, and various corporations. A smaller but equally important portion of her clientele includes advertising agencies, publishers, photographers, and individuals.

Bice's attention to detail is evident in even the simplest of assignments. She has won several awards and has attained national and international recognition with her precise handling of the airbrush. Her goal is to produce work that surpasses the technical expectations of her clients, while creating a piece of artwork that satisfies the spirit's need to soar.

PROJECT
Hot Steel, Private Collection
RENDERING SIZE
13" x 17" (33 cm x 43 cm)
MEDIUM
Marker

PROJECT
Oakchia, Private Collection
Limited Edition Fine Art Print

RENDERING SIZE
24" x 36" (61 cm x 91 cm)

MEDIUM
Watercolor

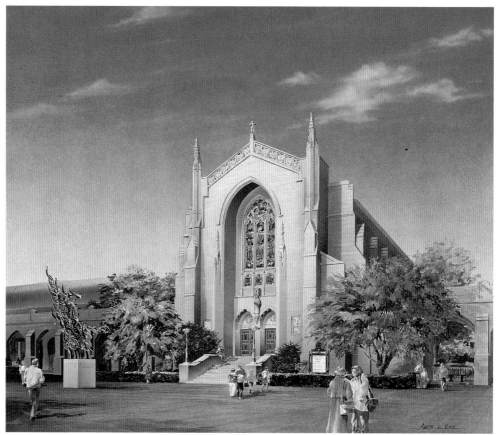

PROJECT
Marsh Chapel
New Horizons Ltd., Birmingham,
Alabama

RENDERING SIZE
16" x 18" (41 cm x 46 cm)

MEDIUM
Airbrush, watercolor

PROJECT
The University of the South
Sewanee, Tennessee
Private Collection

RENDERING SIZE
16" x 20" (41 cm x 51 cm)

MEDIUM
Watercolor

PROJECT
Parisian, Phipps Plaza
Atlanta, Georgia

CLIENT
KPS Group Inc., Birmingham, Alabama

RENDERING SIZE
24" x 36" (61 cm x 91 cm)

MEDIUM
Airbrush

PROJECT
Proposed Renovation, Dallas Mills
Huntsville, Alabama

CLIENT
KPS Group Inc.
Birmingham, Alabama

RENDERING SIZE
24" x 36" (61 cm x 91 cm)

MEDIUM
Airbrush, watercolor

PROJECT
Family Life Center
Assemblies of Brethren Church
Nassau, Bahamas

CLIENT
Roger F. Cartwright, AIA
Birmingham, Alabama

RENDERING SIZE
20" x 24" (51 cm x 61 cm)

MEDIUM
Airbrush, watercolor

BOOKS/PERIODICALS

Illustration Index, Volumes I & II
Page One Publishing, Singapore

Airbrush Action I, II, & III,
Design Library: Airbrush, Rockport
Publishers, Rockport, Massachusetts

*The Encyclopedia of Airbrush
Techniques* by Michael E. Leek,
Quarto Publishing, London

*Southern Living's Quick Decorating;
American Country Christmas 1995;
Sew Easy, Sew Now; Quick Stitch
Quickies,* Oxmoor House Inc.,
Publisher

Baptist Today Magazine

Airbrush Action Magazine,
Competition winner 1989, 1990,
1991, 1992, 1993

Southern Accents Magazine

Healthy Choice Magazine

PROJECT
Cutaway, Recovery Boiler
for Paper Mill

CLIENT
BE&K Engineering,
Birmingham, Alabama

Townsend, Bentley
Ad1 Advertising Agency
Birmingham, Alabama

RENDERING SIZE
24" x 36" (61 cm x 91 cm)

MEDIUM
Airbrush on film positive

PROJECT
Architectural Pediment, *Baptist Today*
Britton Advertising, Montgomery, Alabama

RENDERING SIZE
4" x 12" (10 cm x 30 cm)

MEDIUM
Airbrush

PROJECT
Window Detail, Oxmoor House Inc., Publisher
Birmingham, Alabama
RENDERING SIZE
12" x 14" (30 cm x 36 cm)
MEDIUM
Watercolor

CLIENT LIST

BE&K Engineering, Birmingham, AL

Britton Advertising, Montgomery, AL

Evan Terry Associates, Birmingham, AL

Fortinberry & Associates, Birmingham, AL

Gresham Smith & Partners, Birmingham, AL

KPS Group, Birmingham, AL

Turner Batson Architects, Birmingham, AL

The Ritchie Organization, Birmingham, AL

Canizaro Trigiani Architects, Jackson, MS

Oxmoor House, Birmingham, AL

Southern Accents *Magazine, Birmingham, AL*

Parisian Department Stores, Birmingham, AL

Sain Associates, Birmingham, AL

*UAB Architecture and Engineering,
Birmingham, AL*

Harbert International, Birmingham, AL

City of Birmingham, Birmingham, AL

David Jones, Jr., Architects, Birmingham, AL

Tur Architects, Florence, AL

*Tucker Wayne/Luckie Advertising,
Birmingham, AL*

Jesse J. Lewis Advertising, Birmingham, AL

Ballard Covert Group, Birmingham, AL

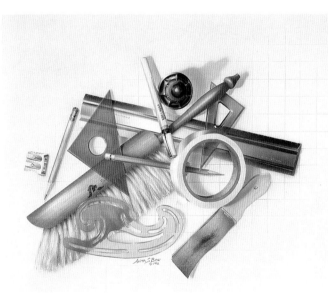

PROJECT
On the Drawing Board
"Baptist Today"
Britton Advertising
Montgomery, Alabama
RENDERING SIZE
13" x 15" (33 cm x 38 cm)
MEDIUM
Airbrush

PROJECT
Working Back From Injury
Montgomery Rehab.
Hospital,
Britton Advertising
Montgomery, Alabama
RENDERING SIZE
12" x 26" (30 cm x 66 cm)
MEDIUM
Airbrush

13-B PAULINE STREET
WINTHROP, MA 02152
617-846-4766

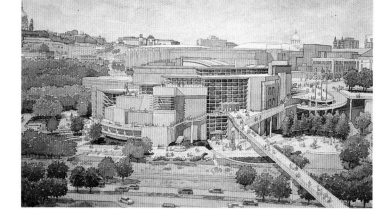

PROJECT
Science Museum of Minnesota
St. Paul, Minnesota
CLIENT
Ellerbe Becket
Minneapolis, Minnesota
RENDERING SIZE
11" x 17" (28 cm x 43 cm)
MEDIUM
Watercolor

Frank M. Costantino

In a process of discovery compatible with the architect's creation of form, the work of Frank M. Costantino has achieved a level of professional distinction by fashioning unique perspective interpretations to his clients' designs. The evolving design imagery of any given project is sensitively addressed and convincingly portrayed in the apparent space, time, form, and color of an illustration.

Whether the creative expression in perspective is sought at the conceptual, design development, or construction drawing phases, F.M. Costantino Inc. offers a wide variety of drawing responses to effectively serve architecture's aesthetic and functional purposes. The firm's scope of work, lengthy list of satisfied clientele, and expanded portfolio of award-winning and internationally exhibited illustrations are qualitative assets in striving for an uncompromising degree of excellence. Fourteen artworks have been jury-selected for *Architecture In Perspective* Exhibitions, AIP II, III, IV, V, VI, VII, VIII, IX, X, and XI, 1987–1996.

The finer matter of Mr. Costantino's efforts is attaining an artistic level of arresting visual message. Such a worthy goal must be resourcefully sought in the composition and color studies of a drawing; in the color palette choices of pencil, watercolor, pen and ink, or other medium; in the texture of vellum, paper, film or mylar. A fluid drawing process for combining these elements, applied in an economy of means with an economy of experience, assists the image in magically manifesting itself before the eyes. With mastery comes facility; with facility comes freshness; with freshness comes a vigor of discovery; therein lies the excitement, pleasure, and satisfaction of the architectural drawing.

Further examples of Mr. Costantino's artwork can be seen in *Art of Architectural Illustration 1*, *Architectural Design Collaborator's Sourcebook 1, 2, & 3*, as well as many published texts in the field.

PROJECT
Hancock Tower Axial 1
Boston, Massachusetts
RENDERING SIZE
10" x 13" (23 cm x 33 cm)
MEDIUM
Watercolor

In addition to the opportunities for personal drawing expression afforded by receptive clients, this portfolio's project drawings were produced with the expert assistance of Arthur Dutton, M.Planning, Harvard University; Michael O'Beirne, B.F.A., B.Arch., Rhode Island School of Design; and Judith Pradell, B.F.A. Emmanuel College, B.Arch, Boston Architectural Center.

PROJECT
Liberty Tower
Jakarta, Indonesia

CLIENT
Ellerbe Becket
New York, New York

DESIGN PARTNER
Peter Pran
New York, New York

RENDERING SIZE
12" x 22" (30 cm x 56 cm)

MEDIUM
Verithin colored pencils
on mylar with computer
image

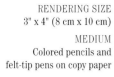

RENDERING SIZE
3" x 4" (8 cm x 10 cm)

MEDIUM
Colored pencils and
felt-tip pens on copy paper

RENDERING SIZE
6" x 11" (15 cm x 28 cm)

MEDIUM
Colored pencils and
felt-tip pens on
sketch trace

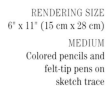

RENDERING SIZE
6" x 11" (15 cm x 28 cm)

MEDIUM
Colored pencils and
felt-tip pens on
sketch trace

RENDERING SIZE
6" x 10 1/2"
(15 cm x 27 cm)

MEDIUM
Colored pencils and
felt-tip pens on
sketch trace

In the process of resolving and interpreting the design intent, a series of nineteen preliminary drawings became an essential asset to the designers and the illustrator to effectively compose the final watercolor image of dense wildlife.

PROJECT
Tsuruhama Rainforest Pavilion, Osaka, Japan

CLIENT
Cambridge Seven & Associates

EXHIBIT DESIGNER
Lyons Zaremba, Boston, MA

RENDERING SIZE
13" x 21" (33 cm x 53 cm)

MEDIUM
Watercolor

HONOR AWARD SELECTION
Architecture in Perspective 10

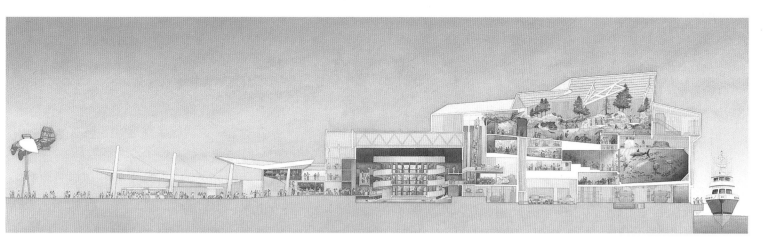

PROJECT
New England Aquarium, Boston, Massachusetts

CLIENT
Schwartz/Silver Architects, Boston

EXHIBIT DESIGNER
Lyons Zaremba, Boston, Massachusetts

RENDERING SIZE
28" x 82" (71 cm x 208 cm)

MEDIUM
Watercolor

PROJECT
Mittra City Center, Jakarta, Indonesia

CLIENT
Ellerbe Becket, Minneapolis, Minnesota

RENDERING SIZE
11" x 17" (28 cm x 43 cm)

MEDIUM
Watercolor

This in-house sketch painting was completed with the design
team in two days for a presentation to Indonesia's president.

PROJECT
San Francisco Museum of Modern Art
San Francisco, California

CLIENT
San Francisco Museum of Modern Art

ARCHITECT
Mario Botta

RENDERING SIZE
8" x 10" (20 cm x 25 cm)

MEDIUM
Watercolor for Premier Edition note
card series

Frank M. Costantino　31

PROJECT
Vassar College Observatory, Rochester, New York

CLIENT
Roth and Moore, New Haven, Connecticut

RENDERING SIZE
9" x 14" (23 cm x 36 cm)

MEDIUM
Graphite pencils on Lana watercolor paper

At the artists' suggestion, the college and architect agreed on an appropriate starlight setting, but also on the wintry, shadowy environment, which the jury observed ". . . has a magical quality and provides a reminder of a child-like experience with observatories and constellations . . . it is very persuasive. Despite the chilly aspect created by the elements of winter night and moonlight, the drawing artfully captures the sensual and romantic."

PROJECT
Vassar College Observatory
Rochester, New York

CLIENT
Roth and Moore, New Haven, Connecticut

RENDERING SIZE
6" x 9" (15 cm x 23 cm)

MEDIUM
Graphite pencils on tracing paper

A two-hour sketch image to convince the college of the illustration approach.

PROJECT
Corporate Headquarters
Riyadh, Saudi Arabia

CLIENT
Zeybekoglu Neyman Associates
Cambridge, Massachusetts

RENDERING SIZE
12" x 11" (31 cm x 28 cm)

MEDIUM
Verithin colored pencils on mylar

PROJECT
Concert Hall Stage, Kuala Lumpur, Malaysia
CLIENT
Cesar Pelli & Associates, New Haven, Connecticut
RENDERING SIZE
8" x 10" (20 cm x 25 cm)
MEDIUM
Pastel and wax-based pencil on Xerox vellum

PROJECT
Boylston Street Commons, Boston, Massachusetts
CLIENT
Jung Brannen, Architects, Boston, Massachusetts
RENDERING SIZE
13" x 16" (33 cm x 41 cm)
MEDIUM
Wax-based pencils on photo mural of pencil drawing

Rua do Alto da Milha, 50A
São João do Estoril, 2765
Portugal
+351-1-467-1010/466-0624
+351-1-466-1648 fax

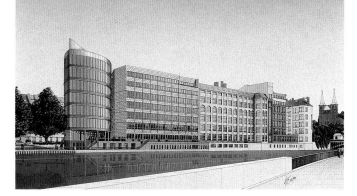

PROJECT
Spree Forum, Berlin, Germany
ARCHITECT
Jan & Prof. Josef Paul Kleihues
Berlin
CLIENT
Hanseatica, GmbH
RENDERING SIZE
16" x 10" (41 cm x 25 cm)
MEDIUM
Airbrush on schöeller paper

PROJECT
Office Building
Setúbal, Portugal
ARCHITECT
Sua Kay, Lisbon
RENDERING SIZE
10" x 16" (25 cm x 41 cm)
MEDIUM
Airbrush on schöeller paper

Angelo DeCastro

Angelo DeCastro is an architect who has been dedicated exclusively to the work of architectural perspectives since 1985. Based in Lisbon, Portugal, he has been working closely with architects, engineers, construction companies, and real estate and marketing agencies throughout Europe and Brazil, his native country.

DeCastro's primary work is to create different angles of the building from the computer. This provides a variety of choice for the client, creates a base for the final perspective, and helps him to achieve accurate results.

Working in all available media—including graphite, prismacolor, pen and ink, watercolor, and markers—DeCastro's realistic airbrushed images are a specialty. Being an architect, he thinks it is important to represent architecture with all its details and precision.

PROJECT
Syntec Park
Tennenlohe, Germany
ARCHITECT
Friederich & Partner
Seeheim, Jugenheim
CLIENT
Revalor, GmbH
RENDERING SIZE
33" x 20" (84 cm x 51 cm)
MEDIUM
Airbrush on schöeller paper

ANGELO DE CASTRO - 10/92

PROJECT
Colonade Plaza
Berlin, Germany

ARCHITECT
Prof. Hans Kollhoff, Berlin

CLIENT
Hanseatica, GmbH

RENDERING SIZE
16" x 10" (41 cm x 25 cm)

MEDIUM
Airbrush on
schöeller paper

PROJECT
Hypo Bank
Neubrandenburger, Germany

ARCHITECT
Prof. Hans Kollhoff, Berlin

RENDERING SIZE
16" x 10" (41 cm x 25 cm)

MEDIUM
Airbrush on schöeller paper

PROJECT
Wohn Park, Nauen, Germany

ARCHITECT
Heinz Fahrenkrog-Petersen
Berlin

CLIENT
Hanseatica, GmbH

RENDERING SIZE
16" x 10" (41 cm x 25 cm)

MEDIUM
Airbrush on schöeller paper

PROJECT
Colombo Shopping Center
Lisbon, Portugal

ARCHITECT
RTKL International, Dallas, Texas
José Quintela da Fonseca, Lisbon

CLIENT
Sonae Imobiliária SGPS, SA

RENDERING SIZE
24" x 10" (61 cm x 25 cm)

MEDIUM
Airbrush on schöeller paper

PROJECT
Aga Khan Foundation
Lisbon, Portugal

ARCHITECT
Raj Rewal, New Delhi
Frederico Valsassina, Lisbon

RENDERING SIZE
16" x 10" (41 cm x 25 cm)

MEDIUM
Airbrush on schöeller paper

PROJECT
Shopping Center & Stadium Flamengo
Rio de Janeiro, Brazil

ARCHITECT
Coutinho, Diegues & Cordeiro, Rio de Janeiro
Ellerbe Becket, New York

CLIENT
Combracenter Shopping Centers, SA

RENDERING SIZE
16" x 10" (41 cm x 25 cm)

MEDIUM
Airbrush on schöeller paper

PROJECT
Portugal Telecom Building
Competition Expo '98
Lisbon, Portugal

ARCHITECT
José Luiz Quintino, Estoril

RENDERING SIZE
10" x 16" (25 cm x 41 cm)

MEDIUM
Airbrush on
photographic paper
Building: Computer image

PROJECT
Goya Building
Lisbon, Portugal

ARCHITECT
João R. Paciência, Lisbon

CLIENT
BBV Imobiliária

RENDERING SIZE
16" x 10" (41 cm x 25 cm)

MEDIUM
Airbrush on
schöeller paper

AFFILIATIONS

Member, American Society of Architectural Perspectivists; Representative in Portugal

Member, The Portuguese Association of Architects, Portugal

Member, The Brazilian Institute of Architects, Brazil

PUBLICATIONS

The Art to Illustrate Architecture, *Rio de Janeiro, November 1995*

Architecti, *March 1995*

Immobiliaria, *July 1994*

AIP10, ASAP *Catalog, October 1995*

EXHIBITIONS

The Art to Illustrate Architecture I, Rio de Janeiro, May 1992

Architecture in Perspective 10, Seattle, October 1995; honorable mention with the work "Spree Forum," Berlin, Germany

The Art to Illustrate Architecture II, Rio de Janeiro, November 1995

PROJECT
Lisbon Towers
Lisbon, Portugal

ARCHITECT
Frederico Valsassina, Lisbon

RENDERING SIZE
16" x 10" (41 cm x 25 cm)

MEDIUM
Airbrush on schöeller paper

PROJECT
Mundial Hotel, Lisbon, Portugal

ARCHITECT
João Vasconcelos Marques, Estoril

RENDERING SIZE
16" x 10" (41 cm x 25 cm)

MEDIUM
Airbrush on schöeller paper

PROJECT
Norte Shopping
Rio de Janeiro, Brazil

ARCHITECT
Designcorp Ltd., Toronto
Lindi Ltda, Rio de Janeiro

CLIENT
Center Norte, SA

RENDERING SIZE
17" x 12" (43 cm x 30 cm)

MEDIUM
Airbrush on
schöeller paper

430 EAST 20TH STREET, 5B
NEW YORK, NEW YORK 10009
212-260-4240

PROJECT
La Caixa Headquarters
CLIENT
I.M. Pei & Partners
RENDERING SIZE
21" x 16" (53 cm x 41 cm)
MEDIUM
Acrylic

PROJECT
E.M.C. Headquarters
Des Moines, Iowa
CLIENT
Brooks Borg & Skiles
RENDERING SIZE
16" x 20" (41 cm x 51 cm)
MEDIUM
Acrylic

Lee Dunnette, AIA

Trained in history and philosophy, Lee Dunnette is an architectural illustrator equipped for special projects. He is experienced in all aspects of the design process, with ten years as a registered architect in New York City and membership in AIA, ASAP, and NYSR. He has seven years' experience with 3-D CAD, "ray trace" rendering, computer graphics, and color plotting. As this portfolio shows, Mr. Dunnette is also a master at capturing drama and visual poetry. After all, architecture is both "frozen music" and visual joy!

PROJECT
Tower Competition, Guangehou, China
CLIENT
Lee Timchula
RENDERING SIZE
16" x 16" (41 cm x 41 cm)
MEDIUM
Acrylic

PROJECT
The Pyramid at Le Grand Louvre
1995 ASAP Hugh Ferriss Memorial Prize

CLIENT
I.M. Pei & Partners

RENDERING SIZE
30" x 16" (76 cm x 41 cm)

MEDIUM
Acrylic

PROJECT
Symphony Hall
Kuala Lumpur, Malaysia

CLIENT
Cesar Pelli & Associates

RENDERING SIZE
21" x 16" (53 cm x 41 cm)

MEDIUM
Acrylic

PROJECT
Terminal One
John F. Kennedy International Airport
New York, New York

CLIENT
William Nicholas Bodouva Architects

RENDERING SIZE
24" x 12" (61 cm x 30 cm)

MEDIUM
Acrylic

PROJECT
Al Jeraisy Headquarters
Riyadh, Saudi Arabia

CLIENT
Cesar Pelli & Associates

RENDERING SIZE
12" x 27" (30 cm x 69 cm)

MEDIUM
Acrylic

PROJECT
Union Block East
New York, New York

ARCHITECT
Lee Dunnette

RENDERING SIZE
23" x 30" (58 cm x 76 cm)

MEDIUM
Freehand ink, airbrush

PROJECT
Madison Arcade
New York, New York

ARCHITECT
Lee Dunnette

RENDERING SIZE
19" x 19" (48 cm x 48 cm)

MEDIUM
Pastel

PROJECT
Newport Coast Resort, California

CLIENT
Aldo Rossi/Studio di Architectura

RENDERING SIZE
16" x 11" (41 cm x 28 cm)

MEDIUM
Freehand ink, airbrush

New Denver International Airport
Airside Concourses   Concourse Holdroom

714 First Avenue West
Seattle, Washington 98119
206 282-8785
206 282-8764 fax

Bill Evans

PROJECT
Denver Airport (Interior)
Denver, Colorado

Mr. Evans works in a broad range of techniques, from loose conceptual sketches to finished rendering in line, line and color, to transparent or opaque watercolor. He feels that the proper ambience and a good artistic feel are the main elements of a successful drawing. The correct light, shade, color, sense of activity, and setting must be brought together with the architecture to produce a quality rendering.

Bill's approach to illustration is to produce a blend of art and technique. To that end, Mr. Evans is continually refining his skills through sketching and fine-art painting. Bill is also producing computer-generated illustrations combining his rendering, drawing, painting, and computer skills

PROJECT
Denver Airport (Interior)
Denver, Colorado
ARCHITECT
T. R. A.
CLIENT
United Airlines
MEDIUM
Opaque watercolor

New Denver International Airport
Airside Concourses   Central Core Atrium

PROJECT
Westlake Union Center
Seattle, Washington

ARCHITECT

NBBJ

RENDERING SIZE
26" x 18" (65 cm x 45 cm)

MEDIUM
Opaque watercolor

PROJECT
Seattle Waterfront
Cruise ship terminal
Seattle, Washington

ARCHITECT
Hewitt Isley

CLIENT
Port of Seattle

RENDERING SIZE
18 x 26" (45 cm x 65 cm)

MEDIUM
Transparent Watercolor

PROJECT
Kangbok Medical Facility
Kangbok, Korea
Competition winning entry

ARCHITECT
NBBJ

RENDERING SIZE
17" x 17" (43 cm x 43 cm)

MEDIUM
Transparent watercolor

PROJECT
Church of the Epiphany
Seattle, Washington

ARCHITECT
Elsworth Story (Original)
L. M. N. Architects (Remodel)

RENDERING SIZE
15" x 15" (38 cm x 38 cm)

MEDIUM
Transparent watercolor

PROJECT
Watercolor painting

RENDERING SIZE
20" x 25" (51 cm x 63.5 cm)

MEDIUM
Watercolor

PROJECT
Portugal
Watercolor painting

RENDERING SIZE
16" x 24" (41 cm x 61 cm)

MEDIUM
Watercolor

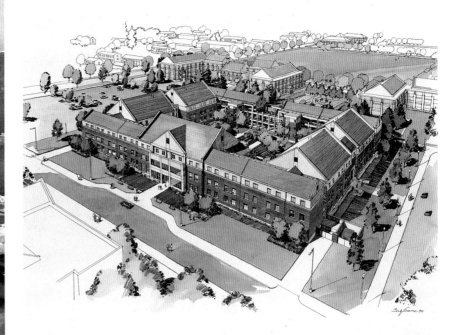

PROJECT
Military Barracks
Ft. Louis, Washington

ARCHITECT
WJA Architects

RENDERING SIZE
18" x 28" (46 cm x 71 cm)

MEDIUM
Graphite line
and watercolor

PROJECT
Landing Mall
Port Angeles, Washington

ARCHITECT
L. M. N.

RENDERING SIZE
17" x 24" (43 cm x 61 cm)

MEDIUM
Graphite and watercolor

Bill Evans　**49**

PROJECT
Line Sketches

RENDERING SIZE
@ 11" x 17" (28 cm x 43 cm)

MEDIUM
Ink on paper

PROJECT
Auld House

ARCHITECT
Stewart Silk

RENDERING SIZE
15" x 25" (38 cm x 63 cm)

MEDIUM
Graphite

PROJECT
Line Sketch, Seattle Symphony
Seattle, Washington
ARCHITECT
L.M.N.
RENDERING SIZE
18" x 26" (46 cm x 66 cm)
MEDIUM
Graphite

PROJECT
Sketches, Bars and Restaurants
Seattle, Washington
RENDERING SIZE
17" x 17" (43 cm x 43 cm)
MEDIUM
Ink line

The Essential Idea:

A Building is not a Drawing
By Thomas W. Schaller, AIA

"It is not enough to see architecture, you must experience it," writes S.E. Rasmussen, meaning that we cannot truly know a building merely by studying images of it.

The truth of this statement lies in the fact that a building's nature primarily resides in its three-dimensional tangibility, its corporeal identity, and its use. But it must be remembered that experiencing an architectural painting is not the same as seeing or experiencing a building. Each serves a different goal and has a different function: separate but valid experiences sharing a commonality of language, but responsive to different and equally compelling, creative voices.

The assertion that a building is not a drawing may strike the reader as obvious. Yet autonomy, in the disciplines of architectural design and architectural design graphics, is often and understandably obfuscated. That a building can come to exist independent of architectural drawing is not so much the question, but rather "how successfully may it do so?" In theory, a building could be constructed without the aid of drawings. In most cases, this is not an advisable (or even legal) practice.

So, while a building is not a drawing, a building may not be particularly sound, aesthetically pleasing or efficient without drawings. The acts of building and drawing may be inseparable, yet it would be a mistake to see one discipline service to the other. For while the interdependence of the practice of architecture (the business of building), and the process of architecture (the act of designing) is known and well-documented, the independence and viability of architectural artwork as an end in itself is somewhat less obvious and certainly less well-appreciated.

A completed building is deemed worthy or unworthy regardless of the various forms (concept development sketches through construction documents) of architectural graphics employed to help it come about. Similarly, an example of architectural artwork can succeed or fail strictly upon its own merits regardless of any specific building it may represent. Two related—but essentially different—artistic impulses are at work in the creation of the three-dimensional object and the two-dimensional idea.

A valid notion of the independence between various forms of artistic expression comes from Malraux in his book, *Voices of Silence,* in which he states

> to the eyes of the artist, things are primarily what they may come to be within that privileged domain where they "put on immortality" but for that very reason, they lose some of their attributes: real depth in painting, real movement in sculpture.

This process is identified by Malraux as reduction and called the very beginnings of artistic expression: to create art, one is forced to choose and is willingly limiting oneself to the two dimensions in painting; in music, the strictly aural, and in architecture, the lack of abstraction. The artist's vision is formed early, feels Malraux, and conditioned by the objects or ideas of his or her passion. For instance, the sculptor is most deeply moved by status, the painter by paintings, the architect by buildings. In youth, the "more deeply moved by his visual experiences of works of art than by that of the things they represent."

This deeply important distinction is illustrated by Malraux, who cites the landscape painter who sits down to paint a sunset over the sea as an example. While a reasonably faithful representation of the scene may be produced, the painter's efforts are ultimately informed far more by painting than they are by the natural surroundings. The red of the sky and the blue of the water may be used as inspiration, but it is the color of the pigments that are used as elements in a separate, viable world, which is created brushstroke by brushstroke upon the canvas. While it may be said that the painting springs from nature, it is important to remember that painting is not nature, nor is nature painting. The artist's voice exists, perhaps in tandem with, but separate from, the elements of inspiration. Therefore, a painter of seascapes is not necessarily one who is primarily enamored of rocks and water, but one who, above all, loves paintings. Similarly, the architectural artist is one who is primarily moved by the images of architecture. And so, it is the architectural artist's paintings, not the buildings or even the ideas of the buildings which may inform them, which hold the key to the true significance of his or her work.

There are, to be sure, architects who effectively design or study characteristics of building by use of the architectural model only. While it cannot be said that this practice is wrong, the three-dimensional miniature is by nature limited in its very tangibility. Only by means of the drawing or sketch can one abstract or isolate the essential idea sufficiently in an attempt to ascertain not only the proposed building's physical character, but it's spirit, the "feeling" it may eventually inspire in the viewer. This expressed duality, the synthesis of the corporeal and the spiritual, the objective and the subjective, is what the preeminent architectural artist of our century, Hugh Ferriss, termed the "entire truth" about architecture; and the communication of which he felt should be the ultimate goal of the architectural artist.

For Ferriss, this truth, this essential idea, consisted of both information and interpretation. Architectural information is inherently more simple for most of us to attempt to portray graphically—the characteristics of brick, stone, steel, and glass. Yet, since architecture is a three-dimensional art form, it is insufficient for the artist to attempt to merely render physical facts upon the two-dimensional page. Ferriss felt that it was incumbent upon the architectural artist to attempt to visually represent something of the feeling, the spirit, the essence of these building materials. Though certainly no stranger to the demands of "real" architecture, Ferriss was cognizant of the difference between the commu-

nicative properties of buildings and those of drawings. For the contemporary architectural artist, regardless of medium or subject matter, there are substantial lessons to be learned in the works of Ferriss. Through a gauntlet of sophisticated commercial architectural specificity and constraint, shines the light of inspiration—the essential idea—with astonishing clarity.

No, a building is not a drawing, but neither is a drawing a building. While knowledge of the ideas and elements of design may certainly be essential for the artist to produce a better architectural drawing, so too, facility with the necessities of graphic communication cannot help but to assist the architect in producing a better building. And it stands that the aspiring designer who "thinks with a pencil" (whether that takes the form of an actual pencil, a paintbrush or a computer screen) may have a greater opportunity to produce a valid work of art than one who does not.

THE PERFECT DRAWING

For those of us who have spent our lives in pursuit of the "perfect" drawing, one natural and understandable assumption is that we must therefore learn to draw perfectly. Armed with this naive and inductive conclusion in mind and a pencil or paintbrush in hand, a lengthy journey commences for the would-be artist. Thinking perfection must somehow lie in knowledge and expertise, we see on the landscape a daunting series of technical and intellectual obstacles to surmount; a pursuit to which an entire career could be easily devoted, at the end of which, if we travel the course successfully, we presume we will be rewarded with knowledge or ability.

Unfortunately, these hurdles, even if systematically and perfectly mastered, may not hold the key to allowing the artist to possess the skills required to execute even the palest shadow of perfection. There is something missing, something which even with years of study, one may still not produce.

Determining what constitutes the "perfect" drawing (of architecture or any other subject matter) ought, perhaps, to be the first avenue of study. The answer to this mystery may not lay in study, at least not in the form of study that involves more and more advanced technical or intellectual acuity. A glimpse of an answer rather may be found in an appreciation of the drawings of the untrained child. The differences between the visual representations of a child and those of a skilled adult are apparent enough. However, what may not be evident is that the adult's work, no matter how polished or accomplished, is not necessarily better. The child's work may display a certain lack of definition, perhaps an oversimplification of detail or what may appear to be a lack of understanding of proportion and perspective. The adult's efforts in turn, especially when distinguished by years of study and practice, can certainly achieve a finesse, a "completeness" and a sophistication. But it is the seemingly intangible emotive aspects of a child's drawing that are lacking in the work of more highly trained individuals. It is the uncanny ability of a child to represent something in its purest, simplest, and yet most surprisingly complete and telling form. It is the error of the adult mind to equate perceived completeness with "correctness"—technical complexity with absolute superiority. In fact, the drawings of some children display remarkable insight, skill, and completeness within their own frames of reference, which are not necessarily uncomplex. They share the ability to capture that "essential idea": Ferriss's touchstone for the "truth."

When a child reaches for a pencil or paintbrush, the results more often appear to be an attempt at self-expression than an exercise in representation. But what adults may see as a child's "incomplete" way of seeing or of representing are in fact simply an "alternative" way. A child often seems to feel more readily than to think; what a child paints or draws is by definition often far more subjective and personal than what might be produced by many a professional artist or draftsperson. The child's drawing represented here is the author's young nephew's graphic response to a conversation on the topic of drawing a forty-story building. Having rarely, if ever, seen one firsthand, it is a surprisingly successful attempt on the artist's part at distilling the essence of an idea.

Noted writer on the psychology of artistic response, Rudolph Arnheim, feels that despite appearances and arguments to the contrary, children do in fact draw what they see, but more importantly, not necessarily all they see. They know something that endless study and academic pursuit can rarely teach the adult maker of images: when to quit. Children seem to know what to put in and what to leave out. They know when a picture is finished. A drawing by a child may be simple not necessarily in betrayal of any lack of perception, insight or absence of skill, but because, according to Arnheim, "it fulfills all the conditions he expects the picture to meet." In this light many so-called naive works begin to appear brave, skillful, and communicative. And it is in their clarity and directness that many more mature efforts at visual representation begin to pale.

Arnheim asserts that perception begins with the general and proceeds to the specific. It does not, in his view, commence with specifics that are abstracted into generalities by the intellectual process. So then, it may be in this way that a

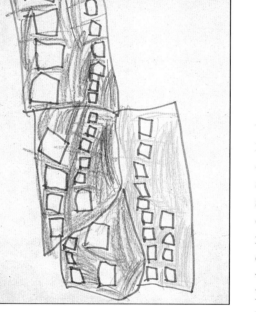

child's drawing can astound even more than it can charm in its ability to both grasp and represent the general, the essential. It is this ability, lost to most adults through years of education, that can make their attempts at visual representation, while perhaps rich in technical skill and intricate detail, so wanting in spirit and, ultimately, in substance.

It can be convincingly argued that while the professional's work is, in some ways, closer to perfection, the child's work may be closer to art. This realization must encourage anyone seriously pursuing some form of "perfection on paper" to turn a critical eye inward. The "perfect" drawing may therefore be an amalgam of the emotion and the intellect, the subjective and the objective, the perfect and the imperfect: Ferriss's "entire truth."

A final observation from Arnheim's work with children's drawings is that the act of drawing or painting (and incidentally architecture itself) differs from photography in that it comes about sequentially. It is—not unlike the very process of perceptual development itself—a cumulative art, built up in stages. The result, not necessarily the process, is seen and judged all at once. This is especially critical for the artist to comprehend and remember since, at heart, it contains the truth that art is not so much in the paint, as it is in the act of painting; in other words, the process is as, if not more, important than the product. Therefore, if the process is true to the initial conception then it must follow that the product will result in enhancing rather than obscuring that essential idea. This need to understand the sequentiality of human creative endeavor was further illustrated by Arnheim via the writings of Baudelaire, who said that

a good painting, faithful and equal to the dream that gave birth to it, must be created like the world. Just as the Creation we see is the result of several creations, of which earlier ones were always made more complete by the next, so a painting, if handled harmoniously, consists of a series of superimposed pictures, where each new layer gives more reality to the dream and makes it rise another step toward perfection.

What, therefore, may be viewed as a child's incomplete, undeveloped or limited way of seeing can just as easily be assessed as an alternative way of seeing. These drawings may well hold clues to an invaluable method of perception lost to most adults, even those involved in the day-to-day business of picture-making. Moreover, it should be apparent that the most successful drawings, regardless of their subject matter or relative level of skill, are a synthesis of the subjective and emotional accessibility of the child and the objective and more intellectual investigation of the adult.

So when, as would-be artists, we turn our eye to the depiction of an architectural subject, it is crucial to remember that it is not the building, but the essence of the building which must be discerned, interpreted and portrayed. At least as much effort should be expended in discovering the exact nature of that elusive quality as is spent in perfecting any graphic technique or medium.

Eventually we see that it is necessary to discover the "painting within the *idea*" of a building. And it may be literally through the eyes of a child that we, as trained adults, can at last become able to learn those elusive skills that make our efforts at the drawing table begin to communicate an essential idea—the "entire truth" of Ferriss—and approach the ideal.

PROJECT
The Chicago
Tribune Tower

RENDERING SIZE
19.5" x 12.25"
(49 cm x 31 cm)

ARTIST
Hugh Ferriss

Courtesy of Avery
Architectural and
Fine Arts Library,
Columbia University,
New York

P.O. Box 326
The Sea Ranch, CA
95497
707-785-2184
800-233-0658
707-785-2264 Fax

PROJECT
Chemistry Building
University of Washington
CLIENT
Moore Ruble Yudell
RENDERING SIZE
14" x 17" (36 cm x 43 cm)
MEDIUM
Watercolor

PROJECT
California Center for the Arts
Escondido
CLIENT
Moore Ruble Yudell
RENDERING SIZE
14" x 17" (36 cm x 43 cm)
MEDIUM
Watercolor

Al Forster

Al Forster's role as an architectural renderer has always gone beyond the domain of "illustrator." His ability to work during the early conceptual stages of a project has made him a true member of the design team. He has been able to work in a great range of media as well as at many levels of detail. Often his quick sketches of preliminary ideas that are being explored are enormously helpful as feedback in the design process both for the team and for the clients. He is also able to convey with great care the qualities of habitation of the places that are being designed. His watercolor techniques strike a marvelous balance; literal enough to convey a true sense of proportions and materials, yet loose enough to allow the viewer to partake in and to inhabit the places that are being imagined. Working together over a long period of time has also allowed us to collaborate more seamlessly. Al Forster's work and process have exemplified an extraordinary range of work from loose and diagrammatic to precise and descriptive as the occasion requires.—Buzz Yudell

"Charles Moore" A. Forster '91

PROJECT
Competition, First Place
Maryland Center for Performing Arts
CLIENT
Moore Ruble Yudell
RENDERING SIZE
10" x 15" (25 cm x 38 cm)
MEDIUM
Watercolor on line sketch

PROJECT
Ritter Hall
Replacement Facility
Scripps Institution of
Oceanography

CLIENT
Hardy Holzman Pfeiffer,
Design Architects;
Ehrlich-Rominger,
Executive Architects

RENDERING SIZE
22" x 30" (56 cm x 76 cm)

MEDIUM
Watercolor

PROJECT
Berlinerstrasse Housing
Potsdam, Germany

CLIENT
Moore Ruble Yudell

RENDERING SIZE
14" x 17" (36 cm x 43 cm)

MEDIUM
Watercolor

PROJECT
San Francisco Airport
Competition: Finalist

CLIENT
MBT Architects

RENDERING SIZE
20" x 30" (51 cm x 76 cm)

MEDIUM
Watercolor

PROJECT
Cook County Memorial Hospital
Chicago, Illinois

CLIENT
Bobrow/Thomas and Associates

RENDERING SIZE
24" x 36" (61 cm x 91 cm)

MEDIUM
Watercolor

PROJECT
White Barn, The Sea Ranch
Field Sketches

RENDERING SIZE
5" x 6" (13 cm x 15 cm)

MEDIUM
Watercolor

PROJECT
Santa Fe Station Concourse (Renovation)
San Diego, California

CLIENT
Hannah Olin Ltd., Landscape Architecture
Philadelphia, Pennsylvania

RENDERING SIZE
24" x 36" (61 cm x 91 cm)

MEDIUM
Watercolor

PROJECT
Sculpture Studio
Occidental College

CLIENT
Levin and Associates with
Hodgetts + Fung Architects

RENDERING SIZE
20" x 30" (51 cm x 76 cm)

MEDIUM
Watercolor

PROJECT
The Huntington
Condominium (Detail)

CLIENT
Lorimer/Case

RENDERING SIZE
24" x 36" (61 cm x 91 cm)

MEDIUM
Watercolor

PROJECT
Proposed Animation Studio
Dreamworks SKG

CLIENT
Moore Ruble Yudell

RENDERING SIZE
11" x 17" (28 cm x 43 cm)

MEDIUM
Watercolor on line sketch

PROJECT
Dreamworks Campus

CLIENT
Moore Ruble Yudell

RENDERING SIZE
12" x 18" (30 cm x 46 cm)

MEDIUM
Quick Sketch Watercolor

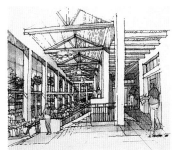

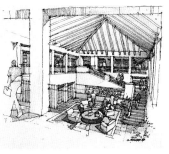

PROJECT
Main Street
Williamsburg Town Plan
Competition

CLIENT
Akai Mingkae Yang and
James Mary O'Connor,
Design Associates

RENDERING SIZE
12" x 15" (30 cm x 38 cm)

MEDIUM
Watercolor on line sketch

PROJECT
Ambulatory Care Center
UC Davis

CLIENT
The Stichler Design
Group Inc.

RENDERING SIZE
20" x 30" (51 cm x 76 cm)

MEDIUM
Watercolor

PROJECT
San Diego Justice Center

CLIENT
Carrier Johnson Wu,
Architect
Robert Davis,
Design Consultant

RENDERING SIZE
24" x 36" (61 cm x 91 cm)

MEDIUM
Watercolor

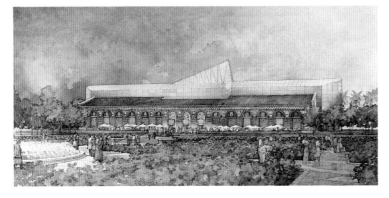

PROJECT
California Museum of
Science and Industry

CLIENT
Zimmer Gunsul Frasca
Partnership

RENDERING SIZE
14" x 20" (36 cm x 51 cm)

MEDIUM
Watercolor

PARTIAL CLIENT LIST

Moore Ruble Yudell, Architects, Santa Monica
Zimmer Gunsul Frasca Partnership,
Los Angeles, Portland
R.L. Binder, FAIA, Playa Del Rey
Bobrow/Thomas Associates, Los Angeles
Carrier Johnson Wu, San Diego
Ehrlich, Rominger, San Diego
Fehlman, LaBarre, San Diego
Hanna Olin Ltd., Philadelphia
Hardy Holzman Pfeiffer, Los Angeles
Johnson Fain and Pereira, Associates
Killeford Flammang Purtill, Santa Monica
KMA Architecture, San Diego
Levin Associates, Los Angeles
LPA, San Diego, Newport Beach
Lyndon Buchanan, Berkeley
MBT Architects, San Francisco
Neptune Thomas Davis, San Diego,
Corona, Pasadena
Robinson Mills + Williams, San Francisco
The Stickler Design Group, San Diego
William Turnbull Associates, San Francisco
USC, UCLA, UC Berkeley, UC Davis, UC Irvine

PROJECT
Shangh Grand Theater Competition

CLIENT
Moore Ruble Yudell, Architects
Santa Monica

RENDERING SIZE
16" x 22" (41 cm x 56 cm)

MEDIUM
Watercolor on line sketch

GORSKI & ASSOCIATES P.C.
6633 SPOKANE AVENUE
LINCOLNWOOD, ILLINOIS 60646
847-329-1340

PROJECT
World's Tallest Building
Moscow, Russia
Aerial View, Elevation View (inset)
CLIENT
Skidmore Owings & Merrill, Chicago, Illinois
RENDERING SIZE
12" x 19" (30 cm x 48 cm)
MEDIUM
Colored pencil, airbrush

Gilbert Gorski

AWARDS

*Municipal Art Prize, 80th Chicago
and Vicinity Show,
Art Institute of Chicago*

*Honor Award, 1990, Chicago Cultural
Center, "Alternative Visions" Exhibit*

*Honor Award, 1991, American Institute
of Architects, Chicago chapter,
Art by Architects*

*Juror's Award, 1989, 1994, American
Society of Architectural Perspectivists*

*Honor Award, 1987, 1989 through 1996,
American Society of Architectural
Perspectivists*

*Honor Award, 1994, Society of
Illustrators, New York*

*Hugh Ferriss Memorial Prize, 1990,
American Society of Architectural
Perspectivists*

PROJECT
181 East Lake Shore Drive, Chicago, Illinois
CLIENT
Booth, Hansen & Associates, Chicago, Illinois
RENDERING SIZE
17" x 38" (43 cm x 97 cm)
MEDIUM
Colored pencil, airbrush

PROJECT
IRS, Maryland Competition

CLIENT
Kohn Pedersen Fox
Associates, P.C.
New York, New York

RENDERING SIZE
12.5" x 30" (32 cm x 76 cm)

MEDIUM
Colored pencil, airbrush

PROJECT
Science Building
Grinnell College
Grinnell, Iowa

CLIENT
Holabird & Root, Chicago

RENDERING SIZE
14" x 27" (36 cm x 69 cm)

MEDIUM
Colored pencil, airbrush

PROJECT
The Interior of the
Basilica Ulpia
Trajan's Forum, Rome
(second century, A.D.)

COMMISSIONED BY
Archeologist Professor
James Packer
Northwest University

RENDERING SIZE
19" x 26.5" (48 cm x 67 cm)

MEDIUM
Colored pencil, airbrush

PROJECT
Saitama Stadium
Competition
Nikken Sekkei, Japan

CLIENT
Dan Meis, Ellerbee Becket
Santa Monica, California

RENDERING SIZE
16" x 20" (41 cm x 51 cm)

MEDIUM
Colored pencil, airbrush

PROJECT
Saitama Stadium
Competition
Nikken Sekkei, Japan

RENDERING SIZE
14" x 20" (35 cm x 51 cm)

PROJECT
Saitama Stadium
Competition
Nikken Sekkei, Japan

RENDERING SIZE
12" x 18" (30 cm x 46 cm)

PROJECT
840 North Michigan Avenue
Chicago, Illinois

CLIENT
Lucien LaGrange & Associates
Chicago, Illinois

RENDERING SIZE
17" x 32" (43 cm x 81 cm)

MEDIUM
Colored pencil, airbrush

PROJECT
Residential Complex
Ixtapa, Mexico

CLIENT
Skidmore Owings & Merrill
Chicago, Illinois

RENDERING SIZE
12" x 15" (30 cm x 38 cm)

MEDIUM
Colored pencil, airbrush

PROJECT
Major League
Baseball Stadium
Phoenix, Arizona

CLIENT
Ellerbe Becket
Kansas City, Missouri

RENDERING SIZE
16" x 28" (41 cm x 71 cm)

MEDIUM
Oil on canvas

PROJECT
Major League Baseball Stadium
Phoenix, Arizona

RENDERING SIZE
16" x 28" (41 cm x 71 cm)

PROJECT
"Waiting for the Pope"

RENDERING SIZE
46" x 70" (117 cm x 178 cm)

MEDIUM
Oil on canvas

JANE GREALY AND ASSOCIATES
SUITE 7, 322 OLD CLEVELAND ROAD
COORPAROO, BRISBANE, QLD 4151 AUSTRALIA
+61-7-3394-4333
+61-7-3849-0646 FAX

PROJECT
QUT Business Faculty Building
ARCHITECT
Peddle Thorp Architects
RENDERING SIZE
20" x 14" (50 cm x 35 cm)
MEDIUM
Gouache

Jane Grealy

Wherever you are, call and challenge Jane Grealy and Associates. With a well-orchestrated, multidisciplined team on top, they are confident about their product. Jane Grealy and Associates is energized to deliver visual enhancements of their clients' concept proposals that win the day.

Jane Grealy and Associates offer award-winning methodologies that treat their clients as working partners. The firm's rendering styles suit its clients' every need, varying from photographic realism to atmospheric sketches in numerous mediums and delivery techniques.

Technical accuracy, with strict attention to detail are hallmarks of this qualified group, which ranges from architects to industrial designers and graphic designers.

PROJECT
Justice Reigns Though the Heavens Fall
Law Courts Submission
ARCHITECT
Peddle Thorp & Harvey
RENDERING SIZE
39" x 20" (100 cm x 50 cm)
MEDIUM
Gouache

FIAT JUSTITIA ET RUANT COELI

CLIENT LIST

*Commonwealth
Government Australian
Construction Services
Queensland Government
Brisbane City Council
Federal Airports Corp.
M.I.M. Holdings Ltd.
James Hardie Ltd.
Cox Richardson
Architects & Planners
Daryl Jackson Pty. Ltd.
Consolidated Properties
Daikyo Group
Fletchers Construction
Australia Ltd.
Jupiters Casino Ltd.
Lloyds Ships Pty. Ltd.
Bligh Voller Architects
Peddle Throp Architects
The Buchan Group
Architects
Davenport Campbell &
Partners Ltd.
Guymer Bailey Architects
Hassell Pty. Ltd.
A.V. Jennings Homes
Total Project Group*

PROJECT
Brisbane International Terminal Complex
Federal Airports Commission

ARCHITECT
Bligh Voller Architects

RENDERING SIZE
33" x 23" (84 cm x 59 cm)

MEDIUM
Gouache

PROJECT
Brisbane International Terminal Complex
(Full Section) Federal Airports Commission

ARCHITECT
Bligh Voller Architects

RENDERING SIZE
71" x 39" (180 cm x 100 cm)

MEDIUM
Pen and ink with watercolor

PROJECT
Subic Bay Waterfront Village
ARCHITECT
Hassell Pty. Ltd.
RENDERING SIZE
33" x 23" (84 cm x 59 cm)
MEDIUM
Gouache

PROJECT
The Hillside Apartments
Cypress Lakes Resort,
Hunter Valley

ARCHITECT
Cox Richardson
Architects & Planners

RENDERING SIZE
20" x 14" (50 cm x 35 cm)

MEDIUM
Gouache

PROJECT
Proposed Office Building

ARCHITECT
Guymer Bailey Architects

RENDERING SIZE
23" x 17" (59 cm x 42 cm)

MEDIUM
Gouache

PROJECT
Epping Plaza Food Court
Pacific Shopping Centers
(Australia) Pty. Ltd.

ARCHITECT
The Buchan Group

RENDERING SIZE
23" x 17" (59 cm x 42 cm)

MEDIUM
Gouache

PROJECT
Bermagui
James Hardie Design Awards

ARCHITECT
Michael Marsham & Associates

RENDERING SIZE
23" x 17" (59 cm x 42 cm)

MEDIUM
Gouache

PROJECT
Terrica Place

ARCHITECT
Australian Construction
Services

RENDERING SIZE
20" x 14" (50 cm x 35 cm)

MEDIUM
Gouache

PROJECT
Waterfront Residential Development
Bretts Wharf and Consolidated Properties
Partnership

ARCHITECT
Peddle Thorp Architects

RENDERING SIZE
23" x 17" (59 cm x 42 cm)

MEDIUM
Gouache

Jane Grealy 73

GORDON GRICE & ASSOCIATES
35 CHURCH STREET #205
TORONTO, CANADA M5E 1T3
416-536-9191
416-696-8866 FAX

PROJECT
Ayung River Walk
Bali, Indonesia

CLIENT
Forrec Ltd.

RENDERING SIZE
29" x 15" (74 cm x 39 cm)

MEDIUM
Pencil crayon on mylar

Gordon Grice, OAA, MRAIC

For more than 20 years, as principal in the firm Gordon Grice & Associates, Gordon Grice has provided architectural presentation and design consultation to a wide variety of clientele in North America and abroad. Gordon's architectural illustrations have been widely published and exhibited throughout the world. He has served as president and vice president of the American Society of Architectural Perspectivists and currently sits on the Board of Governors of that association. For the past two years, his activities have included providing artistic and design direction on a number of projects for Forrec, a Canadian firm specializing in the design and construction of leisure and entertainment facilities.

Gordon's work is characterized by a careful attention to context.
Accordingly, the drawings have been grouped to reflect this: Cultural and Historical Context: pp.74 and 75; Urban Context: p.76; Extra-Urban Context: p.77; Wilderness Context: p.78; Regional Context (Urban Design) and Mythical Context (Themed Leisure Parks): p.79.

PROJECT
Composite Image for an
Art Deco Theme Park
Antwerp, Belgium

CLIENT
Forrec Ltd.

RENDERING SIZE
16" x 16" (41 cm x 41 cm)

MEDIUM
Ink on mylar

Both drawings on this page weave cultural icons into otherwise non-contextual themed environment proposals.

PROJECT
Mnemotech Shelter, Vittorito
Abruzzi, Italy

CLIENT
Maragna Architect Inc.

RENDERING SIZE
18" x 26 " (46 cm x 66 cm)

MEDIUM
Ink and pencil crayon on mylar

AWARD OF EXCELLENCE
Architecture in Perspective 9, 1994

SELECTED SUBMISSION
AIA convention, Los Angeles, 1994;
Japan Architectural Renderers Association
14th Anniversary Show, Tokyo, 1994;
New York School of Interior Design Show,
New York City, 1995

Commissioned by the architect for an ideas competition, the drawing combines elements of existing topography with references to the history and culture of the region.

Da stranieri, con i loro bambini nati in Canada tornarono come turisti nel loro paese natale. Da stranier, ch'i ti revenieren da turist au leur enis. The story of the lonely immigrant landing on strange shores, from the hill towns of a previous epoch is legendary. La pietra leggendaria stava ancora là, quasi insignificante quando a paragone l'antico della "casetta in Canada". La pret leggendarie steev anchor alloche, scunusciute ai chiù fine à quant sciose l'anteich de la "casett in Canad". The legendary stone still stood, almost insignificant when compared to the pristineness of the "casetta in Canada". Il loro orgoglio è basato sul successo in una terra straniera, successo paragonabile ai miglioramenti compiuti dai paesani lasciati indietro. Come tutt quant anch leure s'afferm uicrene, ma le stess haun fatt i paisen abbandunate. Their pride based on success in a foreign land was dampened by similar improvements achieved by the "paesani" left behind. Anche loro hanno lasciato indietro le vecchie mure ed anche loro aurebbero parlato alle montagne alle vedute, all'aria fresca" ed alla "buona polenta". Anch leure haun lassat le vecchje mure e anch leur muisser parlat alle muntagn, alle vedjute, all'aria fresch e alla bona pulent. They too had left the old walls and they too would talk of the mountains, the views, the "aria fresca" and "una buona polenta..."

Nel centro Italia, a 160 km da Roma, in Abruzzo, ne pendici di un monte, una cartina con A.D.1 tissimo del Bettorrito di BETTORRITO, BETTORITA, hard to accept, regardless Bay of Naples." For all razz, m'miett sempr in da-ti-sempr resonja. stando all'elevato nume vicina Cortino, aurebbe sione del grande confli tribuu Petigne, assumen nome di ITALIA, o ITALIC ale Castel Vecchio Sube the walls have stood in timeless town wall ov eva wall interconnect la font, ma alla fejn c' di m'limet e passa al eunice dalle mappet rappresenta la roca for sizjone mi per la ii

destro della valle della il territorio di Vittorito VITTORRITO, parente stret le variante a tale nome for many, comfort was five dollar prints of the Quand t'affecc alla fer matu, n'pu cala. Ma ll territorio di VITTORITO insiemi a quello della CORFINIUM che in occa a metropoli di tutte le lega italica, col nuovo superneguican (l'attu There on the mountain physical context is a memories of a by-gone Tant vot ju cjeje mal sempr n'jaoz azzar Vittorito, come si topografiche la po-

Sane jeren
Senza nu solde affamet dieser de jesen
Chi caga la via vecchje che la gnove sa quell che bass
ma n'sa quelle che trou, Cusci deceveine i vecchie
La fame eve troppo forte, pe fa' sentej ii piant ch j parient
e j'ameice p'setteman puirtevene 'nente
Trist desteine de gente che 'n s'aiv pregate a nesciune, de gente
che fatiaive dalla mateine alla saire, de gente che quind
cunusciaiv ii sacrefje.
Ma la veite è diute i bass, uoggi piagne
e dumane reide.

©1993 GORDON ECCLE ASSOCIATES

PROJECT
Kongens Nytorv
(Topographic site study)
Copenhagen, Denmark

RENDERING SIZE
12" x 15" (30 cm x 38 cm)

MEDIUM
Ink on bond

PROJECT
St. James Square
Montreal, Quebec, Canada

CLIENT
Zeidler Roberts Partnership
Architects

RENDERING SIZE
15" x 18" (38 cm x 46 cm)

MEDIUM
Ink and pencil crayon on mylar

PROJECT
The Bata Shoe Museum
Toronto, Ontario, Canada

CLIENT
Moriyama and Teshima
Architects

RENDERING SIZE
9" x 13" (23 cm x 32 cm)

MEDIUM
Black Prismacolor
on mylar

PROJECT
Colvista
(a hillside community near
Baltimore, Maryland)

PLANNERS
Design Collective Inc.

RENDERING SIZE
(all drawings)
14" x 20" (36 cm x 50 cm)

MEDIUM
Ink and pencil crayon on mylar

Three drawings from a series
of five intended to explain the
preservation of existing flora
and topography in a large
residential proposal.

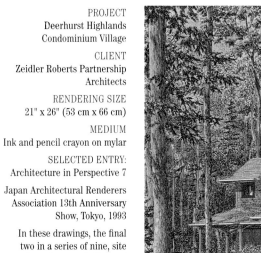

PROJECT
Deerhurst Highlands
Condominium Village

CLIENT
Zeidler Roberts Partnership
Architects

RENDERING SIZE
21" x 26" (53 cm x 66 cm)

MEDIUM
Ink and pencil crayon on mylar

SELECTED ENTRY:
Architecture in Perspective 7

Japan Architectural Renderers
Association 13th Anniversary
Show, Tokyo, 1993

In these drawings, the final
two in a series of nine, site
character was studied and
rendered carefully to convey
the architects' intent to
disturb the site as little
as possible.

PROJECT
Deerhurst Highlands
Condominium Village

CLIENT
Zeidler Roberts
Partnership Architects

RENDERING SIZE
21" x 26" (53 cm x 66 cm)

MEDIUM
Ink and pencil crayon
on mylar

SELECTED ENTRY:
Architecture in
Perspective 8

Japan Architectural
Renderers Association,
14th Anniversary Show,
Tokyo, 1994

Korea Architectural
Perspectivists Association,
Fifth Anniversary Works,
Seoul, 1995

PROJECT
Cultural Centre of the Philippines

CLIENT
Forrec Ltd.

RENDERING SIZE
22" x 32" (56 cm x 81 cm)

MEDIUM
Ink and pencil crayon on mylar

A planning study for a 200-acre tract
in The Philippines. Manila Bay and
some existing buildings provide the
only immediate contextual elements.

PROJECT
Lulu Island Leisure Park

CLIENT
Forrec Ltd.

RENDERING SIZE
10" x 13" (25 cm x 33 cm)

MEDIUM
Ink on vellum

Two sketches in a series of
theme and composition
studies for a leisure park
in the Middle East.

Award of Excellence
(upper drawing)
Architecture in Perspective 10

DIGITAL ARCHITECTURAL
ILLUSTRATION
205 THIRD AVENUE
NEW YORK, NEW YORK 10003
212-677-8054

PROJECT
(both) New Jersey Center
for the Performing Arts
CLIENT
Barton Myers
RENDERING SIZE
8" x 10" (20 cm x 25 cm)

PROJECT
New Jersey Center for
the Performing Arts
CLIENT
Barton Myers
RENDERING SIZE
18" x 24" (46 cm x 61 cm)

Andy Hickes

Andy Hickes practices architectural illustration in Manhattan, specializing in fine electronic renderings. Born and raised in rural Pennsylvania, Hickes earned a Bachelor of Architecture degree from Carnegie-Mellon University, and opened his architectural rendering business in 1978. An active member of the city's professional community, Hickes founded the New York Society of Renderers in 1985. Hickes created all of the images featured here with an Apple Macintosh.

CLIENT LIST
Celebrity Cruises
The Walt Disney Company
Thierry Despont
Ellerbe Becket
Gensler & Associates
Hardy Holzman Pfeiffer Associates
Hellmuth Obata & Kassabaum
Estée Lauder
Lancôme
Pei Cobb Freed & Partners
Planet Hollywood
Peter Pran
Skidmore Ownings & Merrill
Robert A.M. Stern
Takashimya Design
Trump Casino
Rafael Vinoly
Carlos Zapata

PROJECT
Diamond Square multi-use complex
Hong Kong

CLIENT
Brennan Beer Gorman

RENDERING SIZE
30" x 40" (76 cm x 102 cm)

PROJECT
Komplek Kirab RemahjaMulti-use complex
Jakarta, Indonesia

CLIENT
Peter Pran, Ellerbe Becket Associates

RENDERING SIZE
20" x 30" (51 cm x 76 cm)

PROJECT
Casino on Mississippi
Riverboat
St. Louis, Missouri

CLIENT
President Casinos Inc.

RENDERING SIZE
10" x 17" (25 cm x 43 cm)

PROJECT
Exhibition Lobby
Seoul Korea

CLIENT
Rafael Vinoly

RENDERING SIZE
18" x 24" (46 cm x 61 cm)

PROJECT
Atrium for multi-use complex, Hong Kong
CLIENT
Brennan Beer Gorman
RENDERING SIZE
15" x 18" (38 cm x 46 cm)

One of a series of ten drawings

PROJECT
Lancôme cosmetic
installation
Bloomingdale's
Department Store
New York, New York
CLIENT
Lancôme International
Inc.
RENDERING SIZE
20" x 30" (51cm x 76 cm)

PROJECT
Planet Hollywood
CLIENT
Haverson Rockwell
RENDERING SIZE
20" x 30" (51cm x 76 cm)

PROJECT
Internal Revenue Service
National Headquarters
CLIENT
Carlos Zapata
RENDERING SIZE
20" x 30" (51cm x 76 cm)

INTERIOR

1000 HUIZEN
LANGE GEER 44, 2611 PW DELFT
THE NETHERLANDS
31.15.2133382
31.15.2120448 FAX

PROJECT
Sanatorium
Zeist, The Netherlands

CLIENT
Topos Architecten
Waddinxveen

RENDERING SIZE
2" x 3" (5 cm x 8 cm)

MEDIUM
Fineliner, marker, pencil, and pentel correction pen on tracing paper

Willem van den Hoed

Architectural illustration is the communication of a vision from architect to client. The task of the illustrator is to make that vision accessible. Architectural training and artistic flair combine in the work of Willem van den Hoed, from the professional illustrations in which his business specializes to his explorations of architecture in its abstract form.

The key to van den Hoed's approach is flexibility and sensitivity to the landscape and nature. He weaves atmosphere into design, thereby creating the opportunity to observe its future life. Running his own business since 1988 and lecturing on rendering techniques at the Academy of Art, Rotterdam, van den Hoed is a master of a wide variety of techniques. While maintaining that there is power in the precision of detailed graphic images, particularly with the use of color, he is a strong advocate of marker techniques when time is short. Using this technique, it is possible to achieve visual impact within just a few hours.

Complementing van den Hoed's professional work, and inevitably influencing his use of color and perspective in commercial illustrations, is his diary of abstract architecture. Within it, he investigates architectural principles through intuitive forms and colors. He depicts corroded, freestanding volumes with smaller volumes subtracted to create entrances, loggias, and arcades—a playground of poetry in light, color, and dimension. More than images, it is a series of atmospheres where sinister shrouds of oppression and unease sit alongside deserts of serenity and reflection.

Willem van den Hoed uses the diary to challenge the scope of architectural form and to express ideas and observations in an environment without constraints.

PROJECT (ALL)
Restoration of the Anne Frank House
Amsterdam, The Netherlands

CLIENT
Architectenburo Verlaan &
Bouwstra/Temminck Groll

RENDERING SIZE
12" x 12" (31 cm x 31 cm)

MEDIUM
Pencil on paper

PROJECT
Housing
Lelystad, The Netherlands
RENDERING SIZE
8" x 4" (20 cm x 10 cm)
MEDIUM
Marker, fineliner, and pencil

PROJECT
Sanatarium
Zeist, The Netherlands
CLIENT
Topos Architecten, Waddinxveen
RENDERING SIZE
5" x 3" (13 cm x 8 cm)
MEDIUM
Marker, fineliner, and pencil
on tracing paper

PROJECT
Housing Study
CLIENT
Topos Architecten, Waddinxveen
RENDERING SIZE
6" x 4" (15 cm x 10 cm)
MEDIUM
Marker, fineliner, and pencil
on tracing paper

PROJECT
Housing
Almere, The Netherlands
CLIENT
Topos Architecten, Waddinxveen
RENDERING SIZE
6" x 4" (15 cm x 10 cm)
MEDIUM
Marker, fineliner, and pencil
on tracing paper

PROJECT
Housing
Dordrecht, The Netherlands

CLIENT
Wytze Patijn

RENDERING SIZE
12" x 12" (31 cm x 31 cm)

MEDIUM
Airbrush, marker, and
pencil on board

PROJECT
Sport Facilities For A.F.C. Ajax
Amsterdam, The Netherlands

CLIENT
René van Zuuk

RENDERING SIZE
15" x 10" (38 cm x 25 cm)

MEDIUM
Airbrush, marker, and
pencil on board

PROJECT
Office Building for ENECO
The Hague, The Netherlands

CLIENT
Rau and Partners

RENDERING SIZE
18" x 24" (46 cm x 61 cm)

MEDIUM
Airbrush, marker, and pencil on board

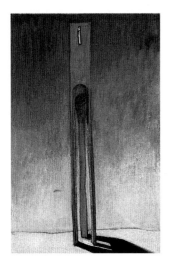

TITLE
Diary I-10

TITLE
Diary I-1, Italian Space

TITLE
Diary II-8

TITLE
Diary III-3

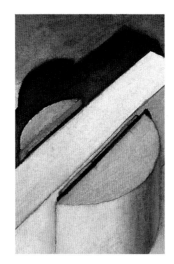

TITLE
Diary II-11

TITLE
Diary II-5

TITLE
Diary IV-9
Housing
Lelystad, The Netherlands

TITLE
Diary III-10

TITLE
Diary IV-7
RENDERING SIZE (ALL)
5" x 3" (13 cm x 8 cm)

MEDIUM (ALL)
Watercolor

RENDERING SIZE
4" x 6" (10 cm x 15 cm)

MEDIUM
Markers on tracing paper

RENDERING SIZE
3" x 4" (8 cm x 10 cm)

MEDIUM
Markers on tracing paper

CLIENT LIST

Architects

Architektenburo Hoogstad, Rotterdam

Architektenburo Haak, Delft

Architektenburo ZZ&P, Amstelveen

LIAG Architekten, Den Haag

Buro voor stadsontwerp Khandekar, Zoetermeer

A+D+P Architekten, Deventer en Amsterdam

Rau & Partners, Amsterdam

TOPOS Architekten, Waddinxveen

Groosman en Partners, Rotterdam

Wytze Patijn, Rotterdam

Project Developers

Domus Vastgoed Ontwikkeling, Woudsend

Amstelland Vastgoed, Rotterdam

Hopman Projektonwikkeling, Zoetermeer

MBO-Ruyters, Maastricht

Fraanje Groep, Ridderkerk

Slokker Vastgoed, Zoetermeer

IJsselbouw, Capelle a/d IJssel

Intervam West, Rijswijk

Other Clients

Zwiers Partners, Rotterdam

Gist-Brocades, Delft

Total Design, Amsterdam

Witteveen en Bos, Deventer

Anne Frank Stichting, Amsterdam

ENECO Den Haag

RENDERING SIZE
6" x 4" (15 cm x 10 cm)

MEDIUM
Markers on tracing paper

827 ½ Via de la Paz
Pacific Palisades, California 90272
310 573-1155
310 573-1685 FAX

PROJECT
Suyoung Bay Competition
Pusan, Korea
Winning Entry
ARCHITECT
Gruen and Associates
MEDIUM
Watercolor

Douglas E. Jamieson

Doug Jamieson is a professional architectural illustrator based in Los Angeles, California, where he has practiced for the past 9 years. Mr. Jamieson holds degrees in both architecture and fine art as well as having years of professional experience in urban planning. This background is invaluable to the client whose project design has yet to be fully realized. As he states, "often the amount of information to proceed with an illustration is a full set of architectural drawings; just as often, however, it is contained on a cocktail napkin."

Well known as a practioner in watercolor, Mr. Jamieson has been exhibited and published worldwide and has garnered many honors and awards including the Hugh Ferriss Memorial Prize in 1992. A fluid expertise with a difficult medium is evident in the exceptional quality of light, color key, and composition displayed in his work. Regardless of his chosen medium, his artwork is characterized by remarkable balance, a strong sense of atmosphere, a timeless quality of style, and a great abstract finesse.

PROJECT
(all this page)

United States
Embassy Competition
Berlin
Winning Entry

ARCHITECT
Moore Ruble Yudell

MEDIUM
Watercolor

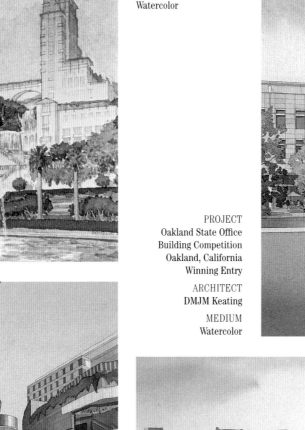

PROJECT
Gazing Heights
Masterplan Competition
Kuala Lumpur
Winning Entry
ARCHITECT
Kaplan McLaughlin Diaz
MEDIUM
Watercolor

PROJECT
Oakland State Office
Building Competition
Oakland, California
Winning Entry
ARCHITECT
DMJM Keating
MEDIUM
Watercolor

PROJECT
Canal City Hakata
Fukuoka, Japan
ARCHITECT
The Jerde Partnership
MEDIUM
Watercolor

PROJECT
Caltrans Proposal
San Francisco
ARCHITECT
Gensler and Associates
MEDIUM
Watercolor

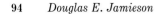

PROJECT
Teltow Housing Masterplan, Berlin
ARCHITECT
Zeidler Roberts Partnership

PROJECT
Kaiser Hospital Proposal
Oakland, California
ARCHITECT
Kaplan McLaughlin Diaz
MEDIUM
Watercolor

SUBJECT
Topographic Studies
Pigeon Key, Florida
MEDIUM
Watercolor

PROJECT
Proposed America's Cup/Louis Vuitton Cup
Commemorative Posters
MEDIUM
Pen and colored pencil studies

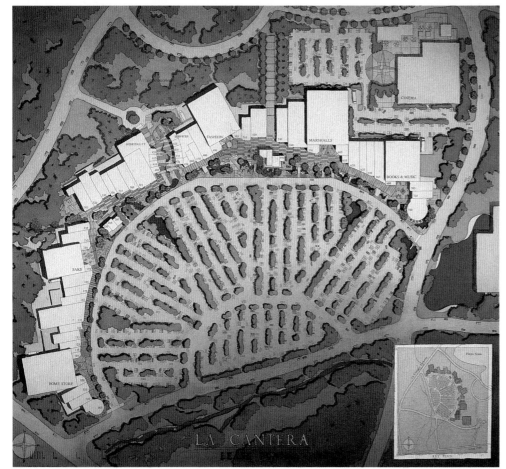

PROJECT
La Cantera Retail Development
San Antonio, Texas
ARCHITECT
The Jerde Partnership
MEDIUM
Watercolor

PROJECT
San Francisco International
Terminal Competition
Winning Entry
ARCHITECT
SOM
San Francisco, California
MEDIUM
Watercolor

PROJECT
Miami International
Airport Concourse
ARCHITECT
Perez and Perez
MEDIUM
Watercolor

CLIENT LIST

Anchen + Allen, Los Angeles, San Francisco

Arquitectonica, Miami

Catellus Development, Los Angeles,
    San Francisco

DMJM Keating, Los Angeles

Dworsky Associates, Los Angeles

Ellerbe Becket, Los Angeles

Gensler Associates, Los Angeles

Gruen Associates, Los Angeles

Hellmuth, Obata + Kassabaum, Los Angeles,
    San Francisco, Hong Kong

Kaplan McLaughlin Diaz, San Francisco

Maguire Thomas Partners, Los Angeles

Michael Wilford and Associates, London

Moore Ruble Yudell, Los Angeles

Moshe Safdie and Associates, Boston

NBBJ, Los Angeles, Seattle

Nikken Sekkei International, Singapore

Pei Cobb Freed & Partners, New York

RTKL Associates, Los Angeles

Skidmore Owings & Merrill, Los Angeles,
    San Francisco, New York

The Getty Museum, Los Angeles

The Jerde Partnership, Los Angeles

Walt Disney Imagineering, Los Angeles

Zeidler Roberts Partnership, Toronto, London

AWARDS

The Hugh Ferriss Memorial Prize
Architecture in Perspective 7, 1992
Jurors Awards
Jean Paul Carlhian Award 1990
Ronald Love Award 1994
Award of Distinction
Architecture in Perspective 10, 1995
Honor Awards
Architecture in Perspective 5, 6, 7, 8, 9, 10;
1990-1995

Drawing to Design;
Drawn Toward Design

By Gilbert Gorski

PROJECT
Steel Corinthian
ARTIST
Gilbert Gorski

My dear! I really must get a thinner pencil. I can't manage this one a bit: it writes all manner of things that I don't intend.

—The White King, Lewis Carroll,
Alice in Wonderland

While most art is created by individuals struggling with themselves, architecture is created by individuals struggling with everybody. Architects orchestrate the efforts of a host of people, and much like composers, their creations are realized through a detailed set of instructions they rely on others to execute. In preparing these instructions they employ instruments or tools that facilitate the process of investigating various possibilities.

Weekend home-repairmen know that the right tool can make the difference between doing a job well or doing it poorly. Tools of different design created to do the same work will impart their own particular character upon that work. This is an important idea and bears repeating; the tools architects use can affect their work, the means by which architects realize their design will affect the architecture itself. Imagine if an architect has only a piece of chalk and a sidewalk to conceive and communicate his or her ideas, the resulting architecture will be much different than if more sophisticated means are used.

Throughout this century, the creation of architectural drawings has never ceased, yet these drawings have been created primarily to document or express ideas and hardly used as tools to explore and predict. In *The Architecture of the Ecole des Beaux-Arts*, Arthur Drexler authors an article suggesting that the lack of humanistic scale in our recent buildings can be attributed to the profession's reliance on models and abstract linear diagrams to study and communicate design intent. The inference could be drawn that small-scale detail and subtle nuances of form as found in pre-twentieth-century architecture can only be described by a technique having an equal sensitivity.

The technique of drawing has been largely discarded as a serious tool for investigating architecture because early twentieth-century, avant-garde thinking discarded ornamentation and decoration and concentrated more upon materials and massing, which were better studied with models. Wright, Mies, and Corbusier—the masters of the modern movement—all received their early training in the methods of the Beaux Arts, yet the schools that grew up around these individuals disregarded that training. Our generation has lost touch with a working methodology that influenced Western architecture for centuries.

Computers as well as models have come to be relied upon by architects and have allowed for design possibilities that could not be possible without them. However, it may be worthwhile to pause and consider how their use in favor of hand drawing can affect the design process. Some practitioners have professed their preference for models as a tool for exploration. For certain types of architecture this is justified, particularly with glass-clad structures where the effects of reflection and transparency are best predicted by models. It is often true, however, that one who develops a habit is unaware of the side effects. For some architects it seems the misdirected aspiration has been to create wonderful-looking models with only secondary consideration given to how they may translate into buildings. Model-making is a process; just as flowing water takes the path of least resistance, it is true that architects use models through a path of least resistance. For example, since it is convenient to observe models placed upon table-tops, they are usually made to appear most appealing from a bird's-eye perspective, even though few people will ever have such a vantage point when seeing the actual building. Models are never made large enough, for unless they can be constructed full size they invariably convey a false sense of scale. Texture and ornamentation in particular are usually ignored or treated as an afterthought because they are impossible to study with any model less than full size. It can also be questioned how well models serve as a tool for discovery. Since model-making, unlike drawing, is not usually done by the designer, it is an indirect process and is not readily open to invention and discovery. Finally, models are expensive to construct and difficult to change and most architects end up using them as a document of their work rather than as a tool for exploring different possibilities.

Computer usage in the area of design is rapidly evolving, and limitations pointed out today may be overcome tomorrow. One restrictive aspect of computers is the tremendous amount of time required to arrive at a three-dimensional color image. This leads to it being used to document ideas rather than exploring them. An even more challenging problem is the fidelity of detail with the computer image: in depicting texture and ornamentation, it cannot approach that achieved by hand with pencil or watercolor. The reasons for this include limitations of hardcopy output, screen resolution, and software that is not nimble enough when predicting the more subtle effects of light and shadow. For instance, computers typically do not realistically address how reflected light illuminates shadows or how color shifts as light strikes it at different angles and at different times of the day. Some software, such as Lightscape, does a good job with rendering smooth-surfaced materials, but falls short in portraying anything with texture.

The experience of drawing in three dimensions with computers reveals that some forms are easier to draw than others. Curved and undulating surfaces in particular are difficult to draw and hard to read on a monitor. One CAD-knowledgeable designer has remarked that computers have impacted the design process so strongly it is possible to detect which software program had been used for the various new buildings being constructed. While this might seem unbelievable to some, it is not hard to suspect that a design evolved through a computer will bend toward a solution that looks good and is easily managed on a computer.

The late twentieth century has witnessed a pluralistic attitude among architects, with some reconsidering the possibilities of ornamentation and decoration. For those who pursue such a course it can be questioned how successfully their work compares to that of their pre-twentieth-century counterparts. Granted, there are many factors involved, such as the loss of the craftsmen and a general cultural shift toward spending less money on architecture. Yet one factor, less obvious but perhaps more exacting, is that architects have lost their command of a technique to describe such architecture.

In trying to regain the eye and hand of the pre-twentieth-century practitioner, a simple three-step program is suggested here that might at least sensitize architects to the possibilities of this different viewpoint: first, architects must learn to draw in a more precise way so that they can accurately predict how light shapes forms and surfaces; second, the use and knowledge of perspective construction can expand the architect's ability to conceive spatial possibilities;

finally, drawing can provide a means of tapping the subconscious and uncovering more evocative possibilities.

At a recent symposium in Chicago, a professional stone carver remarked that he could readily carve from a Louis Sullivan drawing but had difficulty interpreting contemporary drawings in the same way. The difference is that Sullivan drew form while today's architect's draw edges. Looking at Sullivan's drawings, we find that line was seldom used to describe an edge; tones or shading created by closely spaced pencil strokes convey his perception of form. This is a more realistic means of visual communication. Most modern architectural drawings tend to be rather graphic. Not unlike comic book art, they convey information with lines that trace the edges of the various forms. If we're lucky and it's Sunday there might even be some areas of flat color added for special effect. While this technique might be expedient in describing steel and glass buildings, it is inadequate for describing any type of architecture that has texture or subtle surface manipulations. There have been a number of projects I have been involved with in the capacity of an illustrator when the architect provided elevations, created with lines, that appeared rich and dynamic. When rendered, however, particularly in a technique that is closer to photography or how the human eye sees things, the same design became much less interesting. For example, take an instance when a thin light line or band against a darker field needs to be indicated. A drawing made with lines, or even lines and tone will give an inaccurate impression of how it will appear in reality. Usually a thin band indicated by drawing two parallel lines will, when rendered realistically, appear much thinner and less convincing.

One result of the heavy reliance on drawing and watercolor by the Ecole des Beaux Arts was that the architect gained an enhanced sensitivity to light and shadow and, most importantly, an awareness of how the manipulation of form, even in subtle ways, can dramatically affect the perceived outcome. The method of the school in concentrating on elevation over perspective and standardizing the methods of realistic drawing and painting is an effective way to accurately predict how an idea may appear. Employing drawing in this way also avoids the criticism drawings receive and deserve when they distort our perception with overly stylized or impressionistic techniques. Upon looking at original examples of the school's work, it is all the more

striking that technology has yet to invent a better method for describing the exquisitely ethereal moments architecture can possess.

Another important aspect of drawing is the use of three-dimensional perspectives to sharpen the architect's ability to conceive and predict spatial possibilities. In *Many Masks,* Brendan Gill writes:

> Sullivan and Wright possessed a gift in common that was innate and unteachable....The rare gift I speak of was the ability to conceive plan and elevation as one, to move mentally in three dimensions through the volumes of space that a given project called for and to perceive the proportions of those volumes so directly that almost if by magic—certainly without prolonged and painful effort—plan and elevation can be set down in the two dimensions of a sheet of paper.... It was usually the case with a Sullivan design that it was translated into working drawings with few appreciable differences from his first studies on paper. Wright worked in similar fashion, bragging that once he had a building on paper he was ready to set about furnishing it.

From Edgar Tafel's book as well as Wright's autobiography, we learn that both Unity Temple and Fallingwater, two spatially complex structures, were conceived and worked out entirely on paper without the use of models. One might attribute these feats to Wright's genius. However, Wright's abilities as a draughtsmen, particularly in the art of perspective drawing, are well documented and it could be suggested that the exercise of learning to construct three-dimensional images on paper strengthened Wright's power to think three-dimensionally. Granted, the evidence is anecdotal. But when considering other architects noteworthy for spatially complicated buildings (Le Corbusier, Louis Kahn, Eero Saarinen and Paul Rudolph, to name a few), we find they all had a mastery of perspective drawing and each thought it was important enough that despite their busy practices they found time to do these drawings.

It can be successfully argued that models and computers are more dependable in accurately portraying a three-dimensional object such as a building. There is nothing more effective to convince a skeptic of the accuracy of the unanticipated results of viewing a three-dimensional image than to reveal that it was generated with a computer. Yet the act of creating with models and computers does not teach one to think three-dimensionally in the same way the act of creating a hand-drawn perspective on paper can. Perspective drawing strengthens one, almost forces one to see the possibilities of three-dimensional forms and volumes as they emerge from a two-dimensional surface.

Model construction bypasses that elusive moment when ideas are in a state of flux. Since plans and elevations must exist before the model can be started, the act of constructing them has a limited impact on the exploratory process. Computer use in the design process is still limited in much the same way that models are. A breakthrough with computers that may even exist (although this writer has no knowledge of it), would be software that could allow one to view the simultaneous construction of a three-dimensional image as plans and elevations are drawn. Taking this a step further one could imagine a program allowing one to draw three-dimensionally first and then illustrate the resulting plans and elevations. That would be a tool even hand drawing does not afford. Until technology improves or architects demand more of it, perspective drawing remains a proven and reliable tool. It is a tool that can be mastered, and contrary to what Brendan Gill says, can give architects (especially those who may be untouched by a Frank Lloyd Wright–like genius) the ability to see a three-dimensional world on a two-dimensional piece of paper and, "conceive elevation and plan as one." As the Renaissance architect Alberti exclaimed upon mastering the art of perspective drawing, "At last I can see the world as God sees it."

A third and final activity of drawing to be reconsidered and given its proper importance is the act of sketching. Sketching is one of man's oldest activities and may be his best connection between the conscious and subconscious. Yet how often do modern practitioners use sketching to consciously uncover the subconscious as do artists who use sketching to uncover their ideas? Doodling—the carefree spontaneous placement of lines and marks—should be reconsidered as a more serious activity.

Alvar Aalto's work is a well-documented example of a personal and emotional architecture springing from a creative process that began with sketching. In Aalto's own words he described that process:

> ...the immense number of different demands and component problems constitute a barrier from behind which it is difficult for the architectural basic idea to emerge. I then proceed as follows—though not intentionally. I forget the entire mass of problems for a while, after the atmosphere of the task and the innumerable different requirements have sunk into my subconscious, I then move on to a method of working which is very much like abstract art, I just draw by instinct, not architectural synthesis, but what are sometimes child-like comparisons, and in this way, on this abstract basis, the main idea gradually takes shape, a kind of universal substance which helps me to bring innumerable contradictory components into harmony...

Aalto felt humanity shared a common root of feelings in our subconscious and that architecture and the arts were ways in which we could consciously share in those feelings.

Louis Kahn, Le Corbusier, and, more recently, Michael Graves and Norman Foster have indicated the importance of sketching in their work and have consciously used it throughout their careers. Too often today sketching is merely viewed as a pleasant hobby or idle distraction. On the contrary, it is a powerful tool and its importance in the creative process should be reaffirmed.

Forty years ago, H.S. Goodhart-Rendel wrote,

> ...when architecture again becomes pleasant to draw, many happy draughtsmen will arise to celebrate its restoration.

It might now appear for this idea to come true the reverse situation must occur; architects will have to become interested in drawing for buildings to become interesting to draw. Hand drawing remains an alternative to computers and model construction for investigating design. As our culture is poised upon the brink of the new millennium and we look forward into the future, perhaps a new way of approaching architecture would be to reconsider the tools and methods of the past. Not necessarily to create an architecture of the past, but rather to create an architecture that communicates our humanism as successfully as those architects who have come before us managed to do.

> Arriving at each new city, the traveler finds again a past of his that he did not know he had: the foreignness of what you no longer are or no longer possess lies in wait for you in foreign, unpossessed places. — Italo Calvino, *Invisible Cities*

RIYA Co. Ltd.
1-5-5 406 Tomobuchi Cho
Miyakojimaku
Osaka 534 Japan
06 924 3637

PROJECT
A Museum of Tiles Art
Ohmihachiman, Japan
CLIENT
Kan Izue Architects & Associates
RENDERING SIZE
24" x 17" (61 cm x 43 cm)
MEDIUM
Watercolor

Takuji Kariya

This Japanese architectural illustrator endeavors to make full use of the traditional arts and philosophies of his country. Takuji Kariya's works reveal aspects of the traditional Japanese spirit. Nothing illustrates this more than the use of blank space. "A blank space" in Japanese arts, or "a pause" in Japanese performing arts, typifies rustic simplicity, harmony, purity, and tranquility. He weaves his own sense of harmony into the ideas of an architect who is constantly pursuing valuable work, on the basis of traditional heritage for today's use. Kariya argues that the best time for him is when a creative space enhances this artwork more than he and the architect expected.

PROJECT
Lake Side Laboratory
Shiga, Japan
CLIENT
Z Architects
RENDERING SIZE
27" x 19" (68 cm x 48 cm)
MEDIUM
Gouache

PROJECT
Hutte Kai, Nagano, Japan
CLIENT
Z Architects
RENDERING SIZE
27" x 19" (68 cm x 48 cm)
MEDIUM
Gouache

PROJECT
Kansai Airport
Terminal Building
Osaka, Japan
CLIENT
Renzo Piano Building
Workshop
RENDERING SIZE
30" x 19" (74 cm x 47 cm)
MEDIUM
Watercolor

PROJECT
Sea Side Villages of Japan
Kyoto, Japan
RENDERING SIZE
28" x 14" (70 cm x 34 cm)
MEDIUM
Watercolor

PROJECT
Nishikinohama Project
Osaka, Japan

CLIENT
Kan Izue Architects & Associates

RENDERING SIZE
26" x 14" (65 cm x 36 cm)

MEDIUM
Gouache

PROJECT
The Mountain, Green Praise Competition

RENDERING SIZE
29" x 14" (72 cm x 36 cm)

MEDIUM
Gouache

PROJECT
Day Break Church
Kyoto, Japan
CLIENT
Z Architects
RENDERING SIZE
19" x 21" (48 cm x 52 cm)
MEDIUM
Gouache

PROJECT
Nagano Olympic Memorial Hotel
Nagano, Japan

CLIENT
Z Architects

RENDERING SIZE
18" x 14.6" (45 cm x 36 cm)

MEDIUM
Gouache

CLIENT LIST

Kan Izue Architects & Associates
Renzo Piano Building Workshop
Sakakura Associates, Architects & Engineers
Nihon Sekkei Inc.
Z Architects

3891 BAYRIDGE AVENUE
WEST VANCOUVER
BRITISH COLUMBIA, CANADA
V7V 3J3
604-922-3033
604-922-2393 FAX

PROJECT
Silvan Park
Langley, British Columbia, Canada
ARCHITECT
Dalla-Lana/Griffin
RENDERING SIZE
16" x 23" (41 cm x 58 cm)
MEDIUM
Ink, acrylic

PROJECT
New Jinqiao Plaza
Shanghai, China
ARCHITECT
James K. M. Cheng
RENDERING SIZE
15" x 23" (38 cm x 58 cm)
MEDIUM
Ink, colored pencil

Ronald J. Love

Ronald J. Love Architectural Illustration was founded in New York City in 1967, relocating to Vancouver, Canada, in 1972. Today, it continues to offer architectural illustration services to a distinguished worldwide clientele. The studio produces illustrations, from small sketch vignettes to highly detailed finished renderings in pen, acrylic, watercolor, and colored pencil. Computer wire-frame images are often used for accuracy and to establish viewpoints.

Ron Love's illustrations have been represented in numerous books, periodicals, exhibitions, and have received several awards. His work continues to evolve through constant experimentation in mediums and materials.

Member, American Society of Architectural Perspectivists

PROJECT
Bayshore Gardens, Vancouver,
British Columbia, Canada
ARCHITECT
Hotson Bakker
RENDERING SIZE
20" x 30" (51 cm x 76 cm)
MEDIUM
Watercolor, colored pencil

PROJECT
Glen Rosa School
Kelowna, British Columbia,
Canada

ARCHITECT
Dalla-Lana/Griffin

RENDERING SIZE
17" x 23" (43 cm x 58 cm)

MEDIUM
Ink, colored pencil

PROJECT
New Pointe Terrace
Vancouver, British Columbia,
Canada

ARCHITECT
W. T. Leung

RENDERING SIZE
18" x 26" (46 cm x 66 cm)

MEDIUM
Ink, airbrushed acrylic

PROJECT
Condominium Tower
Singapore

ARCHITECT
Paul Merrick

RENDERING SIZE
12" x 16" (31 cm x 41 cm)

MEDIUM
Ink

PROJECT
Condominium
Vancouver, British Columbia,
Canada

ARCHITECT
W. T. Leung

RENDERING SIZE
19" x 23" (48 cm x 58 cm)

MEDIUM
Ink, airbrushed acrylic

PROJECT
Museum Project

DESIGNER
Ronald J. Love

RENDERING SIZE
7" x 12" (18 cm x 31 cm)

MEDIUM
Ink, pastel, colored pencil

PROJECT
Vancouver Place,
Vancouver, British Columbia,
Canada
ARCHITECT
Paul Merrick
RENDERING SIZE
18" x 26" (46 cm x 66 cm)
MEDIUM
Ink, airbrushed acrylic

PROJECT
Cathedral Competition
Singapore

ARCHITECT
Doray/Seow

RENDERING SIZE
16" x 23" (41 cm x 58 cm)

MEDIUM
Acrylic, gouache

PROJECT
The Meridian, Vancouver,
British Columbia

ARCHITECT
Burrows Huggins

RENDERING SIZE
12" x 15" (31 cm x 40 cm)

MEDIUM
Ink and arcrylic

PROJECT
Le Soleil, Vancouver,
British Columbia

ARCHITECT
Burrows Huggins

RENDERING SIZE
16" x 18" (41 cm x 46 cm)

MEDIUM
Ink and acrylic

PROJECT
Alpenglow
Whistler, British Columbia

ARCHITECT
Paul Merrick/Eng & Wright

RENDERING SIZE
14" x 25" (36 cm x 64 cm)

MEDIUM
Acrylic and gouache

PROJECT
Pelangi Luxury Towers
Johar, Malaysia

ARCHITECT
Hemingway Nelson

RENDERING SIZE
20" x 23" (51 cm x 58 cm)

MEDIUM
Ink, airbrushed acrylic

217 Pine St., Suite 1200
Seattle WA 98101
Seattle 206-621-8936
Portland 503-292-2100

PROJECT
Olympic Tower Details
GRAPHIC DESIGNER
Maestri Design
Seattle, Washington
MEDIUM
Chalk and Pencil

Bruce MacDonald

In his drawings, MacDonald's main concerns are that the images be evocative, that compositionally they satisfy the eye, and that they reveal only so much in order to tell the story of the project. The more they reveal, the less engaging they often seem to be. Realistic views are more explicit but there is always an awareness of trying to reach the right mixture of suggestion and silence to allow the image to be completed, in some degree, by the viewer.

Much of the work takes place in the client's office, the place MacDonald thinks interaction with the design team tends to enrich the pieces. The process begins with rough sketches to define the storyline, and moves to refine the image to comply more and more closely with the message. Education: University of Pennsylvania, MArch; Art Center College of Design, Illustration; Macalester College, BA Biology.

PROJECT
King County Parks
20-year Plan
CLIENT
King County Parks
Department
Seattle, Washington
MEDIUM
Chalk and pencil

PROJECT
University of Cleveland Hospitals
ARCHITECT
Payette Associates
Boston, Massachusetts
MEDIUM
Chalk and Pencil

PROJECT
Inn at Port Ludlow
Port Ludlow, Washington
CLIENT
GGLO, Seattle, Washington
MEDIUM
Watercolor

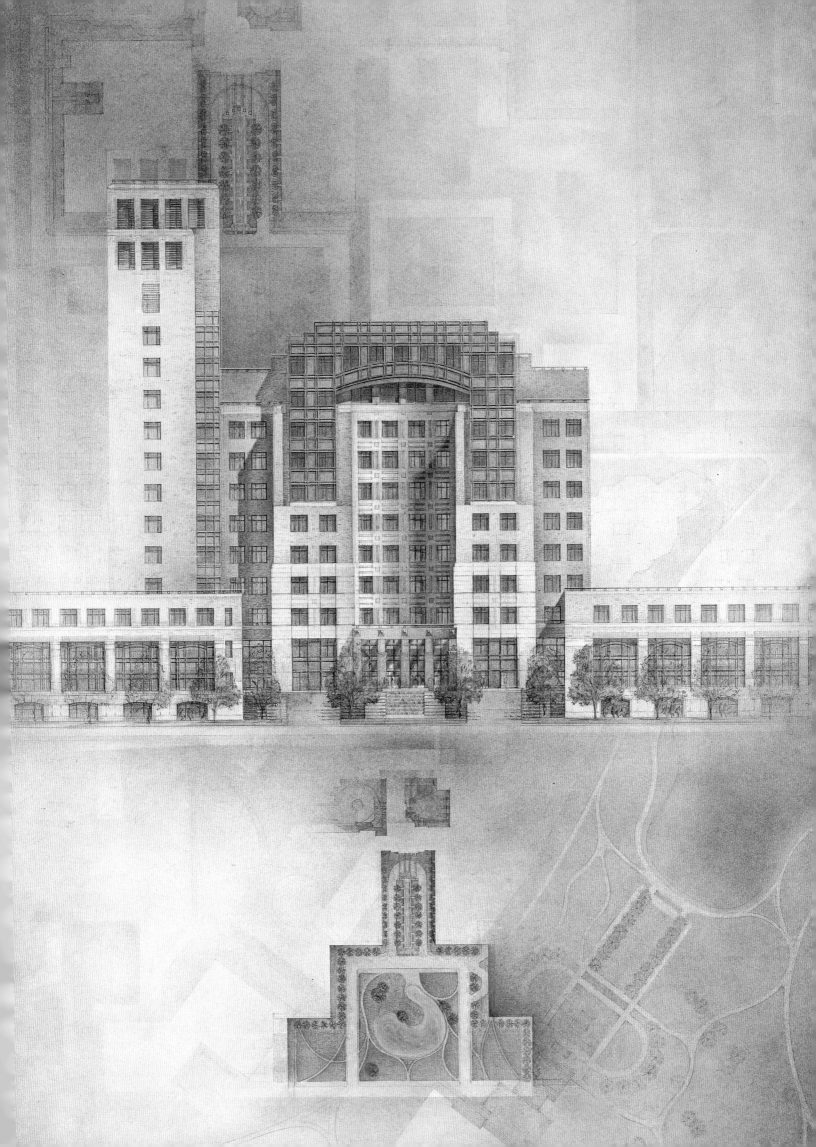

CLIENT LIST

Payette Associates
Graham Gund & Associates
Hemingway Nelson Architects
Waisman Dewar Grout & Carter
Yost Grube Hall Architects
Lee Ruff Stark Architects
SERA Architects
BOORA
Portland Development Commission
The Jerde Partnership, Inc.
Michael Graves Architect
H2L2 Architects
Ballinger
Cooper Robertson Partners
DeMartin Marona Cranstoun & Downes
Zimmer Gunsul Frasca Partnership
GGLO
The Retail Group
NBBJ
Maestri
The Miller Hull Partnership
Kaplan McLaughlin Diaz Inc.
Callison Architecture
The Paramount Theater
King County Parks Department
Interior Design International
CKS Partners

PROJECT
Omni Hotel
New York, New York

CLIENT
Ahearn Schopfer
Boston, Massachusetts

MEDIUM
Pencil on black board

PROJECT
Harborview Hospital
Seattle, Washington

CLIENT
Kaplan McLaughlin Diaz
Seattle Washington

MEDIUM
Chalk and Pencil

PROJECT
Vista House
Condominiums

CLIENT
Yost Grube Hall Architects
Portland, Oregon

MEDIUM
Chalk and Pencil

PROJECT
Cooks Companion

CLIENT
The Retail Group
Seattle, Washington

MEDIUM
Chalk and ink

PROJECT
Inn at Port Ludlow
Port Ludlow, Washington

CLIENT
GGLO, Seattle, Washington

MEDIUM
Watercolor (above)
Marker on trace (right)

PROJECT
Port Coquitlam Law Courts
Port Coquitlam, British Columbia, Canada

CLIENT
Hemingway Nelson
Vancouver British Columbia

MEDIUM
Chalk and pencil

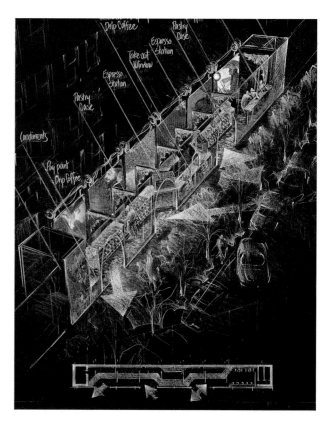

PROJECT
Caravalli Coffees
San Francisco, California

CLIENT
The Retail Group
Seattle, Washington

MEDIUM
Chalk, pencil, found images
on black board

PROJECT
Paramount Theater Interior

DEVELOPER
Ida Cole

MEDIUM
Pencil on black board

PROJECT
Planet Diva Hair Salon

CLIENT
The Retail Group
Seattle, Washington

MEDIUM
Chalk and ink on vellum

PROJECT
Inn at Friday Harbor

CLIENT
GGLO, Seattle, Washington

MEDIUM
Watercolor

PROJECT
Westin Hotel, Seatac Airport
Seattle, Washington

CLIENT
NBBJ, Seattle, Washington

MEDIUM
Chalk and pencil

Bruce MacDonald   119

APA
ARCHITECTURAL PRESENTATION ARTS
43 UNION AVENUE #1
MEMPHIS, TENNESSEE 38103

PROJECT
Jesse Holman
Jones Hospital
Springfield, Tennessee
CLIENT
Gresham Smith Partners
RENDERING SIZE
16" x 30" (41 cm x 76 cm)
MEDIUM
Gouache

PROJECT
Residence Detail
Liberal, Missouri
RENDERING SIZE
9" x 12" (23 cm x 31 cm)
MEDIUM
Oil on paper

Charlie Manus

Charlie Manus has been providing architectural and advertising illustrations for more than 25 years. Illustrating in practically all mediums, his techniques include pencil broadsides, airbrush, colored pencil, and pen and ink (with or without color to full-color illustrations). Manus is also proficient in many types of illustrations including site plans, technical illustrations, vignettes, colored acetates, and scaled elevations. Charlie Manus and Architectural Presentation Arts work closely on a given project throughout all of its phases. Computer wire frames are utilized before any layouts are completed to ensure that there are no questions concerning views. Architectural Presentation Arts also specializes in designing brochures, product mockups, graphic design, signage, and architectural models. Charlie Manus continues to provide illustrations to a prominent and demanding list of regional, national, and international clients.

PROJECT
Jackson Mississippi Children's
Hospital
Jackson, Mississippi
CLIENT
Steve Simmons
RENDERING SIZE
16" x 24" (41 cm x 61 cm)
MEDIUM
Gouache, acrylic

120

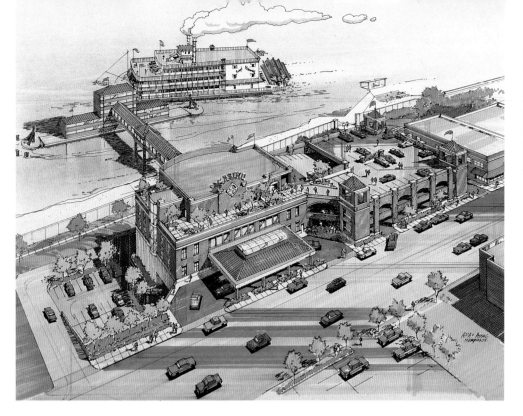

PROJECT
Casino, Cape Girardeau, Missouri

CLIENT
Askew, Nixon, Ferguson Architects

RENDERING SIZE
11" x 17" (28 cm x 43 cm)

MEDIUM
Pen and ink with marker and
watercolor wash

PROJECT
Central Station Renovation
Memphis, Tennessee

CLIENT
JMGR, Inc. Architects and Engineers

RENDERING SIZE
11" x 17" (28 cm x 43 cm)

MEDIUM
Mixed media on mylar

PROJECT
Club House Pickwick Lake
Pickwick Lake, Tennessee

CLIENT
Robert Alexander, Architect

RENDERING SIZE
12" x 22" (31 cm x 56 cm)

MEDIUM
Watercolor wash on paper

PROJECT
Casino, Miami, Florida

CLIENT
Askew, Nixon, Ferguson
Architects

RENDERING SIZE
11" x 17" (28 cm x 43 cm)

MEDIUM
Watercolor wash on paper

PROJECT
Hampton Inn Prototype

CLIENT
Robert Roesler, Architect

RENDERING SIZE
14" x 22" (36 cm x 56 cm)

MEDIUM
Pen and ink on film, airbrush

PROJECT
Trolly Station
Memphis, Tennessee

CLIENT
Hnedak Bobo Group, Architects

RENDERING SIZE
8" x 10" (20 cm x 25 cm)

MEDIUM
Photo retouching, airbrush

PROJECT
Circus Circus Casino
Tunica, Mississippi

CLIENT
Hnedak Bobo Group, Architects

RENDERING SIZE
18" x 34" (46 cm x 86 cm)

MEDIUM
Gouache, acrylic, airbrush

PROJECT
Jubilee Belle Casino
Tunica, Mississippi

CLIENT
Askew, Nixon, Ferguson Architects

RENDERING SIZE
14" x 26" (36 cm x 66 cm)

MEDIUM
Gouache, airbrush

PROJECT
Master Plan
Future Monumental Core Framework Plan
Washington, District of Columbia

PLANNER
National Capitol Planning Commission

RENDERING SIZE
36" x 41" (91 cm x 104 cm)

MEDIUM
Watercolor

PROJECT
Federal Triangle
Future Monumental Core Framework Plan
Washington, District of Columbia

PLANNER
National Capitol Planning Commission

RENDERING SIZE
10" x 14" (25 cm x 36 cm)

MEDIUM
Watercolor

Michael McCann

Michael McCann graduated from the Ontario College of Art in Toronto, in 1968. McCann was awarded a fellowship to The Royal College of Art in London, England, and received the Chalmers Travelling Scholarship. He chose instead to pursue industrial design in Milan, Italy. Having spent a gratifying year there, McCann took a position as a designer with a prominent office in Toronto, Ontario, in 1969. Two years later he formed Michael McCann Associates Ltd., which specializes in architectural presentation.

During the past quarter century, many styles have come and gone. Numerous architects and developers have entered and exited the field, and a broad range of media has been created for a hungry marketplace. The medium of watercolor, however, has remained a staple in architectural presentation. Although watercolor has remained constant in McCann's studio, his dedication to growth through change has allowed techniques to evolve with the changing times. Tight, hard-edged delineations have made way for loose, conceptual drawings, which have in turn opened doors to exciting opportunities outside of the architectural arena. An artist's goal can only be achieved through growth; growth is achieved through dedication and experience.

PROJECT
Aerial Perspective
Future Monumental Core
Framework Plan
Washington, District of Columbia

PLANNER
National Capitol Planning
Commission

RENDERING SIZE
28" x 66" (71 cm x 168 cm)

MEDIUM
Watercolor

PROJECT
East Potomac Riverfront Development
Future Monumental Core Framework Plan
Washington, District of Columbia

PLANNER
National Capitol Planning Commission

RENDERING SIZE
8" x 17" (20 cm x 43 cm)

MEDIUM
Watercolor

PROJECT
Looking East to Washington Monument
Past Lincoln Memorial
Future Monumental Core Framework Plan
Washington, District of Columbia

PLANNER
National Capitol Planning Commission

RENDERING SIZE
8" x 17" (20 cm x 43 cm)

MEDIUM
Watercolor

PROJECT
Osceola Master Plan

CLIENT
Skidmore Owings and Merrill, New York

RENDERING SIZE
12" x 14" (31 cm x 36 cm)

MEDIUM
Watercolor

PROJECT
Arlington Cemetery
Future Monumental Core Framework Plan
Washington, District of Columbia

PLANNER
National Capitol Planning Commission

RENDERING SIZE
9" x 12" (23 cm x 31 cm)

MEDIUM
Watercolor

PROJECT
View from Capital Hill, Looking West
Future Monumental Core Framework Plan
Washington, District of Columbia

PLANNER
National Capitol Planning Commission

RENDERING SIZE
15" x 17" (38 cm x 43 cm)

MEDIUM
Watercolor

Michael McCann **129**

PROJECT
Ravinia Music Festival
Chicago, Illinois
CLIENT
Skidmore Owings and Merrill, Chicago
RENDERING SIZE
11" x 15" (28 cm x 38 cm)
MEDIUM
Watercolor

PROJECT
Girl on Bicycle
Celebration, Florida
DESIGNER
The Walt Disney Company
RENDERING SIZE
8" x 8" (20 cm x 20 cm)
MEDIUM
Watercolor

© Walt Disney

PROJECT
Train Museum
Sentul Raya Square

CLIENT
Skidmore Owings and Merrill, New York

RENDERING SIZE
11" x 14" (28 cm x 36 cm)

MEDIUM
Watercolor

PROJECT
Racetrack Expansion
Rockingham Park, New Hampshire

CLIENT
The Hillier Group,
Princeton, New Jersey

RENDERING SIZE
10" x 16" (25 cm x 41 cm)

MEDIUM
Watercolor

Michael McCann   131

MCILHARGEY BROWN & ASSOCIATES
DESIGN CONSULTANTS & ILLUSTRATION
SUITE 410, 1639 WEST SECOND AVENUE
VANCOUVER, BRITISH COLUMBIA
CANADA V6J-1H3
604-736-7897
604-736-9763 FAX

PROJECT
Johor Coastal Development
Malaysiana and Convention Centre
ARCHITECT
Arthur Erickson Architectural Corp.;
Hijjas Kasturi Associates;
Aitken Wreglesworth Associates;
Atelier M.

Robert McIlhargey/Lori Brown

Robert McIlhargey and Lori Brown have been collaborating as a team for sixteen years. Our office specializes in the design and drawing for visual communication of architectural and planning programs. We also have an extensive background in the design of environmental graphics and signage, and consult on the conceptual design for various projects, including World's Fairs, resorts, and themed attractions.

These assets allow valuable contributions and insights as an integral part of the design and drawing process. Our studio has the capability to consult on the development of multiple drawing portfolios for large projects, such as Al Buhairat City in Saudi Arabia, or alternatively focus on single images to describe structures, architectural, and urban spaces.

The drawings are done in mixed media techniques and range from quick informal pen-and-ink character sketches to fully developed perspectives illustrating major architectural and planning projects. McIlhargey Brown & Associates is a Vancouver-based practice that consults to a diverse and prominent list of clients in the region, nationally, and internationally. We have been members of ASAP since 1987 and have been honoured with numerous awards, participated in national and international exhibitions, and have been in various architectural publications.

PROJECT
Johor Coastal Development

ASSOCIATES

E. RADVENIS
Computer Imaging & Animation

W. WHITE
Project Illustrator

S. McKINNON
Illustrator

Members of American Society
of Architectural Perspectivists

PROJECT
Coca-Cola Oasis Project
Las Vegas, Nevada
DESIGN
Gary Andrishak

PROJECT
Al Buhairat City
Jeddah, Saudi Arabia

PROJECT
Al Buhairat City
Jeddah, Saudi Arabia

ARCHITECT
Aitken Wreglesworth
Associates with Arthur Erickson
Alan Bell Urban Design
& Planning

CLIENT
Al Afandi Establishment

Al Buhairat City is a fully
planned, water-oriented resort/
residential community under
development by the Al Afandi
establishment. It is located on
a 400-hectare site fronting on
the Red Sea and the Gulf of
Salman, just north of Jeddah,
Saudi Arabia. The drawing
portfolio includes 12
townscapes and one
overview drawing.

PROJECT
Coal Harbor Master Plan
Vancouver, B.C.

ARCHITECT
Perkins & Company

CLIENT
ASPAC Developments;
Marathon Realty

PLANNING
Civitas Urban Planners;
R.E. Hulbert Architects

PROJECT
Shanghai Office & Retail
Multiplex
ARCHITECT
James Cheng Architect

PROJECT
Space Center Houston
Visitor's Center
Johnson Space Center
Houston, Texas
ARCHITECT
Architectura
Vancouver, B.C.

Robert McIlhargey/Lori Brown   135

PROJECT
Whistler Town Plaza

ARCHITECT
Perkins & Company

CLIENT
APPIA Developments

PROJECT
Burnaby Arts Centre

ARCHITECT
Hotson Bakker

PROJECT
Mont Blanc Hotel, Whistler, B.C.

ARCHITECT
Perkins & Company

CLIENT
United Properties

PROJECT
Whistler at Christmas

PROJECT
Heavenly Valley Master Plan
ARCHITECT
Design Workshop, Aspen, Colorado

PROJECT
Kalamalka Lake Resort Concept
ARCHITECT
Dowling Knapp

PROJECT
Cuba Resort Concept Plan
ARCHITECT
Civitas Urban Design & Planning

PROJECT
Pin Lin Village River Edge Concept Plan, Taiwan
ARCHITECT
Atelier M/Alan Bell Urban Design & Planning; Arthur Erickson;
Sun-Hsing Architects & Associates

KININGERGASSE 4
1120 VIENNA
AUSTRIA, EUROPE
(0222) 804-43-57

C/O JAMES CAVELLO
578 WEST BROADWAY
NEW YORK, NY 10012
212-925-5700

PROJECT
Government buildings, Zagreb, Croatia
ARCHITECT
Peretti & Peretti
MEDIUM
Watercolor

Morello Design Studio, GMBH

Seeking to offer more than a parochial view of "downtown" nowhere, Barbara Morello has sought projects in Dubai, Zagreb, Moscow, Malaysia, and Washington. Her forte is matching clients' dreams with architects' reality, in detailed watercolors.

With studios in both New York and Vienna, Barbara services an international clientele; fluent in both English and German, she offers a decade of experience, and devotes herself to the quality of each rendering she produces.

PROJECT
Hotel in Bankok, Thailand
ARCHITECT
Housden Barnard, Los Angeles, California
MEDIUM
Watercolor

PROJECT
Train station
Potsdam, Germany
ARCHITECT
William Holzbauer
MEDIUM
Watercolorf

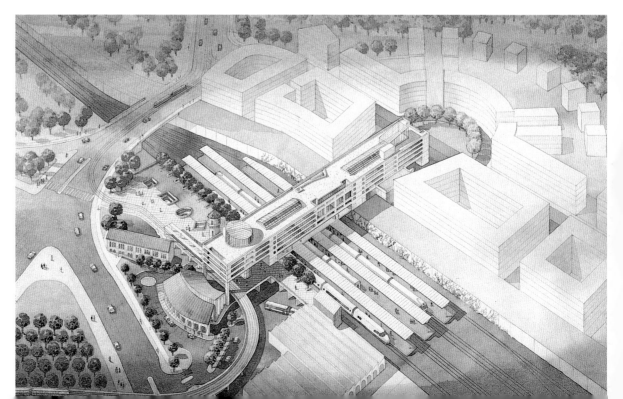

PROJECT
Recovery Hospital
Karschady, Russia

ARCHITECT
Rudolf Scheicher, Salzburg, Austria

MEDIUM
Watercolor

PROJECT
"Vilkerbundpalast in Geneva"
Geneva, Switzerlaqnd

ARCHITECT
Schindler & Neutra, Austria

RENDERING SIZE
21" x 10" (54 cm x 26 cm)

MEDIUM
Watercolor

PROJECT
"Der Spiegel" Competition
in Hamburg, Germany

ARCHITECT
Wilhelm Holzbauer
Vienna, Austria

MEDIUM
Watercolor

PROJECT
Private Residence
Toronto, Canada

ARCHITECT
Steve McCasey, Toronto, Canada

MEDIUM
Watercolor

PROJECT
Plaza Hotel
Moscow, Russia

ARCHITECT
Sutter & Sutter
Basel, Switzerland

MEDIUM
Watercolor

PROJECT (ALL)
Casino Baden, Baden, Austria

ARCHITECT
Peretti + Peretti, Vienna, Austria

MEDIUM
Watercolor

Hand to Mouse

Transition From Conventional To Digital Media: One Renderer's Experience

BY ANDY HICKES

Three years ago, whenever I encountered an article on any computer architectural application, I quickly turned the page, trying to block the idea of using computers for architectural illustration out of my mind. If there were any illustrations resembling renderings, I felt an added sense of dread as I turned the page. Reaching the level of financial and artistic success in my craft at that point was long and difficult, and I had no intention of starting over in another medium. But I felt, and still do feel, change on my heels and gaining.

A friend of a friend had a small, growing graphic design firm where the work was computerized. He had recently graduated from college, and had studied computer graphics. I was surprised and impressed when he told me he had just, one day, bought a computer and taught himself how to use it. My computer was used by others in my office for bookkeeping and word processing. I had not been able to master the programs though I had tried. What follows is from my experience in using computers to render.

THE NEW RENDERING TOOL

There are two general ways to use a computer in rendering. One is as a model builder: after physical dimensions of an object are keyed in, the computer constructs a three-dimensional, mathematical model. This model can be turned and viewed on-screen from any angle. Any view can be rendered and printed. The second way uses the computer as a paint box: the thousands of dots (pixels) on the screen are colored by the computer individually or in selected groups, producing an image on-screen. This image can be rendered at a high-enough resolution to be printed. Modeling programs manipulate the perspective, and paint programs manipulate color and texture. These two techniques can be successfully combined.

Unfortunately, modeling, rendering, and painting software applications are not miracle tools that can make a good illustrator a great one; however, they can be a great boon for the artist. In order to demystify the process, here is a list of some erroneous assumptions many people have about computers:

The computer is a great time saver. This may be true for some people, but it is easy to spend more hours to complete a commission on the computer than using traditional techniques; with a computer it is easy to stay up all night rendering. This is not, however, the fault of the machine. It offers more possible solutions and it takes time to sift through them.

Computers can create beautiful renderings. Clients say they didn't realize a computer could make a rendering this beautiful. The reality is, of course, that it can't. People, using computers, can. This is one of the most difficult things for non-users to really believe. It is not a matter of semantics; there is a subtle, yet powerful, belief in the autonomy of computers, the result of continued marketing of the computer as a wonder machine that can do anything. This marketing strategy is an attempt to assure people who are unskilled with computers that they will be able to easily operate such complex machines. This consoles the unskilled, but subtly implies that we, the skilled, can be easily replaced by any unskilled person using a computer. Computaphobia is deeply ingrained. The illustrator's ability to create by choosing is distinct from the computer's ability to execute those choices. That can be a difficult thing for even a computer user to really believe and remember; only after working with a computer does this distinction show itself.

Computer renderings look different. Most people have seen computer renderings and assumed them to have been done in traditional media. There are programs that mimic charcoal, pastel, and even the most subtle watercolor techniques. Printing the image on high-quality, textured art paper enhances the illusion. Some of today's best-known watercolor renderers digitize the

final hand renderings, then print them on watercolor paper to give the client.

Learning to use a computer to render is difficult. It is easy for most people to learn today's programs. These programs assume little or no experience with computers. A college-student assistant of mine rendered a complete school project after assisting me part-time only several months. His professors, knowing he had little previous computer experience, did not believe he could have done the work alone.

Scanning is as easy as Xeroxing. I myself started by scanning a completed rendering into the computer. I reworked some details with a paint program, drawing and painting as usual but with the computer. On my second computer project, I painted only the building on board using conventional media, then scanned the board. Using the computer, I added sky, trees, and people (scanned previously). After having my computer a month, I colored a scanned perspective sketch completely on screen. Three years later, I am still learning the potential of the computer, finding it easy to use, and still enjoying it.

Clients are interested in digital rendering. Most new clients say they don't want a "computer look," having the same misconceptions listed here. Some people are more open to education than others.

A computer user needs a computer temperament. Architectural illustrators do not have to be interested in computers in general; they can be only interested in the computer's graphics applications and still succeed. Color theory is the basis of a paint program, and no matter what media we work in, we make decisions on brightness, contrast, hue, and saturation instinctively in our work. The paint program precisely delineates these so they can be delicately manipulated independently or in combination.

Systems on which professional quality work can be done are expensive. "Buy the biggest and best you can afford" is good advice, but remember the computer system is just a tool. You don't need the most expensive tools to create excellent work. Beautiful work can be done on systems that cost less than $3,500, including the scanner. Most illustrators have their work printed at service bureaus since, high-quality, large-format color printers still cost more than $50,000.

ADVANTAGES

In general using a standard tool has great advantages. Our small field benefits as the resources of all fields are directed toward improving that one tool. The modeling and painting programs I use are also in standard use in most other fields.

The creative process is one of discovery, fueled by experimentation. After working twenty hours in the traditional methods on an illustration due tomorrow, there's no time to try something new, if it might result in an irreparable mistake. On-screen, there's freedom to experiment without fear of reprisal, because you can always revert to the previous stage. This is why, sometimes, the computer doesn't save time. Since working on screen does not require the same physical stamina as hand work, we can spend more time searching for the effects that work best. More importantly, you can experiment in ways not possible with conventional media. The point in the process when the rendering is near completion can be the most rewarding time to experiment; the overall contrast, brightness or saturation can be manipulated. Or, for example, you can select only the blues and adjust them in any way. Or you can add more yellow to adjust the highlights, and more purple to only the shadows. Even the overall dimensions of the drawing can be changed easily at any time.

Client changes must cause most of the anguish in our work. On a digital rendering you can make any change with relatively little effort. A chair can be moved across the room, or all of the maple wood can be changed to mahogany. Any area can be adjusted independent of the rest of the drawing.

Moreover, since the work is reprintable, the

renderings output for our portfolios will be of the same quality that the client received, not just a photo reproduction. In fact, it's usually of more finished quality; refinements that didn't get done before the deadline can be added when there's time.

Exposure to art supplies and their fumes can be dangerous. Digital work is clean, and free of the chemical fumes that come with traditional airbrushes. Work areas no longer need be a mess of paints and inks; clothes don't need to be stained and ruined. For illustrators whose eyesight is worse for wear after years of close work and who find it a struggle to use an X-Acto knife or ruling pen even occasionally, the computer can "zoom in" and magnify the smallest details on-screen.

DISADVANTAGES

In the short term, expect to see virtuosity outpacing good design. This has already occurred in graphics, general illustration, and typography. These fields switched to digital technology several years before architecture. For example, many of the new typefaces created on the user-friendly typography programs are fascinating, but illegible.

To produce digital renderings, you need the ability to render, the knowledge to operate a computer, and a method to reliably output your work. At present, getting accurate color printouts can sometimes be difficult, relying as it does on the cooperation of outside service bureaus. Besides the sheer inconvenience of this arrangement, there is the problem of quality control. Imagine a department store display of many television sets together on one wall. These sets are all receiving the same signal but there is great variance in their pictures. Printouts from different printers can have the same variance.

The effects of prolonged exposure to video monitors is not known but I think it is responsible for the speed at which my own eyesight has deteriorated. Monitors are suspected of negatively affecting health.

Traditional art methods may suffer. Commercial use dictates the availability and cost of art supplies; as commercial artists turn to electronic media, price and availability of traditional art supplies will be affected. Already, certain inks and papers that were once common are no longer available. More importantly, many hand techniques may be lost by disuse. Even though the same results in pen-and-ink techniques, for example, can be achieved by working on screen, it is easy to miss the spontaneity and immediacy of the hand technique.

All considered, would I go back to working with paints and inks? Not a chance.

THE FUTURE OF COMPUTERS AND THE ARCHITECTURAL ILLUSTRATOR

The tool is reflected in the creation. Gothic cathedrals were created by balancing stones on top of each other as high as possible. The Seagram's building is a steel reconstruction of flat line drawings created with a triangle and T-square. Soon after the Victorians learned to mass-produce the repeating pattern on fabric, everything was covered with a printed or woven pattern. Now we can create by manipulating whole images and three-dimensional, non-planar forms. Visually we are entering a Baroque age resembling MTV more than the National Gallery Building. Complexity and virtuosity will become the fabric of design.

Architects will design by sketching on-screen in three dimensions, manipulating space and form in real time. They will experiment with different forms, spatial relations, color, lighting, and materials as the design progresses on-screen. The finished design will be a fully rendered, three-dimensional digital model. Designing and rendering will be one again.

Getting nervous? Just remember, it's only a tool. Building and selling 20,000 computers a month adds no more intelligence or sensitivity to the world. That will remain our job.

PAUL STEVENSON OLES, FAIA/
ADVANCED MEDIA DESIGN INC.
ONE GATEWAY CENTER
NEWTON, MASSACHUSETTS 02158
617-527-6790/800-697-4720
617-527-6790 FAX
401-272-6240 FAX
soles@mit.edu

PROJECT
New England Aquarium
Boston, Massachusetts

ARCHITECT
Schwartz/Silver Architects

IMAGE
Layout from photo, black-and-white
rendering, retrocolor: P.S.O.

Paul Stevenson Oles, FAIA/ Advanced Media Design Inc.

PROJECT
One Dallas Center
Dallas, Texas

ARCHITECT
Henry N. Cobb, FAIA/
Pei Cobb Freed & Partners

IMAGE
Initial black-and-white
rendering: P.S.O.; revised
digital image: A.M.D.

As an experienced architect and perspectivist, Paul Stevenson Oles has long been motivated to **draw** to investigate, develop, verify, and celebrate designed form as it will appear when built. To pursue these goals pragmatically with maximum efficacy, he has consistently sought and used the best tools available to the craft. Now that the best tools available for certain—but not all—drawing tasks is the computer, his office has affiliated itself with a very capable and creative digital imaging firm for the purpose of investigating, developing, verifying, and celebrating architecture to a level that was not previously possible. The enormous potential inherent in the combining of chirographic (hand-drawn), photographic, and cybergraphic means is the focus of this current effort to develop and to refine a new phenomenon—that is, a unique, graphically integrated approach to the hybrid imaging of architecture.

PROJECT
Federal Courthouse
Boston, Massachusetts

ARCHITECT
Henry N. Cobb, FAIA/
Pei Cobb Freed &
Partners

IMAGE
3-D modeling:
P.C.F.; black-and-white
rendering,
retrocolor: P.S.O.

PROJECT
Shining Office Tower
Taichung, Taiwan

ARCHITECT
Henry N. Cobb, FAIA/
Pei Cobb Freed & Partners

IMAGE
3-D modeling, initial
digital rendering: A.M.D.;
final black-and-white
rendering: P.S.O.

PROJECT
Shining Office Tower
Taichung, Taiwan

ARCHITECT
Henry N. Cobb, FAIA/
Pei Cobb Freed & Partners

IMAGE
Final retrocolor: P.S.O.

PROJECT
Bank of China World Headquarters
(Preliminary Design)
Beijing, P.R.C.

ARCHITECT
I.M. Pei, FAIA/The Pei Partnership

IMAGE
3-D modeling, black-and-white
digital rendering: A.M.D.;
final black-and-white rendering: P.S.O.

PROJECT
International Business School
Shanghai, P.R.C.

ARCHITECT
Pei Cobb Freed & Partners

IMAGE
3-D modeling, digital black-and-white
rendering: A.M.D.; final black-and-white
rendering, retrocolor: P.S.O.

PROJECT
28 State Street
Boston, Massachusetts

ARCHITECT
Elkus/Manfredi Architects

IMAGE
3-D modeling, digital
rendering: A.M.D.;
value studies,
criticism: P.S.O.

Advanced Media Design Inc. is a digital illustration and animation studio specializing in architectural representation. Partners Richard Dubrow and Jon Kletzien combine their skills to convey their clients design intent through the use of the latest, cutting-edge tools in still and dynamic imaging. The commissions executed in affiliation with Paul Stevenson Oles constitute a fraction of the work of the firm, which also includes fund raising and architectural marketing videos, television news clips, and other still and moving image presentations for a variety of clients.

PROJECT
The Greater Buffalo International
Airport (Exterior)
Buffalo, New York

ARCHITECT
Kohn, Pedersen, Fox Associates

IMAGE
3-D modeling,
digital rendering: A.M.D.

PROJECT
The Greater Buffalo
International Airport
(Interior)
Buffalo, New York

ARCHITECT
Kohn, Pedersen,
Fox Associates

IMAGE
3-D modeling, digital
rendering: A.M.D.

PROJECT
The Hotel at the World
Trade Center
Boston, Massachusetts

ARCHITECT
R. Green, FAIA/The
Stubbins Associates

IMAGE
3-D modeling, digital
rendering: A.M.D.

802 Kipling Way
Weldon Springs, Missouri 63304
314-441-8370

PROJECT
Transworld Dome–St. Louis Stadium
St. Louis, Missouri
CLIENT
HOK, Inc. (St. Louis, Missouri)
RENDERING SIZE
14" x 19" (36 cm x 48 cm)
MEDIUM
Prismacolor

Stephen Parker

Architectural imagery in varied media—and multiple levels of development—provide an exciting challenge to Stephen Parker's professional service as an architectural illustrator since 1979. Parker's professional expertise in many styles has taken him around the world, traveling extensively to produce presentation artwork on location at many clients' requests.

He prefers to work closely with design teams in the initial stages of the design process, at which point his talents help expedite crucial decisions, in addition to producing final artwork.

Parker's work has been displayed in a multitude of national and international exhibits, and in many major publications. He says that his ongoing passion is to draw and paint creatively and enthusiastically.

PROJECT
Transworld Dome–St. Louis Stadium
St. Louis, Missouri
CLIENT
HOK, Inc. (St. Louis, Missouri)
RENDERING SIZE
10" x 32.5" (25 cm x 83 cm)
MEDIUM
Prismacolor

PROJECT
Queen City Square
Proposed Office Tower
Cincinnati, Ohio

CLIENT
HOK, Inc. (St. Louis, Missouri)

RENDERING SIZE
33" x 18.5" (84 cm x 47 cm)

MEDIUM
Prismacolor

155

PROJECT
Konkuk Hospital Competition
Korea

CLIENT
HOK, Inc. (Los Angeles, California)

RENDERING SIZE
14" x 20" (35 cm x 50 cm)

MEDIUM
Watercolor

PROJECT
Jing Sheng Plaza
Beijing, China

CLIENT
HOK, Inc. (St. Louis, Missouri)

RENDERING SIZE
18" x 13.5" (46 cm x 34.5 cm)

MEDIUM
Watercolor and Prismacolor

PROJECT
Saltillo Civic Center Proposal
Saltillo, Coahuila, Mexico

CLIENT
HOK /Terrazas, Inc. (Mexico City, Mexico)

RENDERING SIZE
10" x 18" (25 cm x 46 cm)

MEDIUM
Watercolor

PROJECT
Huangpu District Master Plan, Proposal,
Shanghai, China

CLIENT
HOK, Inc. (Shanghai, China)

RENDERING SIZE
11" x 31" (28 cm x 79 cm)

MEDIUM
Watercolor

PROJECT
Cleveland Federal Reserve Bank
Cleveland, Ohio

CLIENT
HOK, Inc. (St. Louis, Missouri)

RENDERING SIZE
18" x 23.5" (46 cm x 59 cm)

MEDIUM
Prismacolor

PROJECT
The New York
Hospital Expansion
New York, New York

CLIENT
HOK, Inc./TCA
New York, New York

RENDERING SIZE
11.5" x 26.5"
(29 cm x 67 cm)

MEDIUM
Prismacolor

PROJECT
Sinar Slipi Sejahtera–PNS
Conceptual Master Plan
Jakarta, Indonesia

CLIENT
HOK, Inc. (St. Louis, Missouri)

RENDERING SIZE
13" x 8" (33 cm x 20 cm)

MEDIUM
Watercolor

PROJECT
Cheng Kung Library Proposal
Tainan, Taiwan

CLIENT
HOK, Inc. (St. Louis, Missouri)

RENDERING SIZE
13" x 7" (33 cm x 18 cm)

MEDIUM
Watercolor

PROJECT
Beijing Housing Development
Beijing, China

CLIENT
HOK, Inc. (St. Louis, Missouri)

RENDERING SIZE
12" x 10.5" (31 cm x 27 cm)

MEDIUM
Watercolor

PROJECT
Puebla New Town
Concept Master Plan
Puebla, Mexico

CLIENT
HOK/Terrazas, Inc.
(Mexico City, Mexico)

RENDERING SIZE
6.5" x 8" (17 cm x 20 cm)

MEDIUM
Watercolor

PROJECT
Abjar Hotel & Beach Club
Dubai, United Arab Emirates

CLIENT
HOK, Inc. (St. Louis, Missouri)

RENDERING SIZE
7.5" x 7.5" (19 cm x 19 cm)

MEDIUM
Watercolor

PROJECT
Lily Pond at Monet's Garden
Travel Sketch
Giverny, France

RENDERING SIZE
8.5" x 5" (22 cm x 13 cm)

MEDIUM
Watercolor

AWARDS

Awards of Excellence in the Graphic Representation of Architecture:

Architecture in Perspective VI, VII, IX, X: 1991, 1992, 1994, 1995

Central States Region AIA Awards, 1993

St. Louis AIA Design Awards, 1994

E.V. Radvenis Inc.
410-1639 West 2nd Avenue
Vancouver, B.C.
V6J 1H3 Canada
604-736-5430
604-736-9763 fax

Eugene Radvenis

E.V. Radvenis Inc. offers the following presentation and visual analysis services to the architectural design and development community:

Mixed-media perspective rendering and illustration—with more than 20 years of experience in architectural design and architectural rendering, E.V. Radvenis Inc. has developed an unique style of architectural illustration that combines various media to communicate an architectural concept to the intended audience effectively.

Computer modeling and image processing—E.V. Radvenis Inc. combines state-of-the-art microcomputer technology with architectural design and illustration skills. This produces 3-D computer models of varying complexity and degree of realism, from simplified massing models useful for design visualization and analysis, to photorealistic fully rendered images that become architectural illustrations in their own right. These computer-modeled images can be further enhanced by combining them with photographic images or backgrounds and using computer image-processing tools to montage the images into an existing context.

Computer animation—E.V. Radvenis Inc. produces video animations of computer models that use motion to explain and explore these simulated architectural environments. The viewer is taken along camera paths that move over, around, and through the model. Objects within the model can be animated for added realism. Subtle effects of lighting and shadow casting can also be explored. The animations are recorded onto videotape and can be combined with live video and sound, resulting in a compact, portable, and captivating presentation package.

PROJECT (ALL)
Simon Fraser University
Conference Center
Exterior and Interior views; retrofit
of a neo-classic bank building
Vancouver, B.C.

ARCHITECT
Architectura

PROJECT
Kuwait Oil Sector Complex
Boardroom Interior

CLIENT
Arthur Erickson Architectural
Corporation in association with
Al-Marzouk and Abi-Hanna WLL;
Kuwait Ministry of Public Works

PROJECT
Kuwait Oil Sector Complex
Typical Office Reception

CLIENT
Arthur Erickson Architectural
Corporation in association with
Al-Marzouk and Abi-Hanna WLL;
Kuwait Ministry of Public Works

PROJECT
Pranin family residence (Interior)
Santa Rosa, California

CLIENT
The Hulbert Group International
Vancouver, B.C.

PROJECT
Water approach to a residential
tower
EXPO lands, Vancouver, B.C.

CLIENT
Concord Pacific Developments Ltd.

PROJECT
Marketing animation,
Al-Buhairat resort development
Red Sea, Saudi Arabia
ARCHITECT
Aitken Wreglesworth Associates,
with Arthur Erickson

Al-Buhairat City is an extensive resort community currently being developed on the desert coast of the Red Sea. It consists of a canal system connected to the Sea, with high-end residential units along the canals. Although Al-Buhairat City is primarily a residential seaside resort, it is also a real city with two distinct commercial zones.

The first, the city center, located in the physical center of the resort and the mainland access to the resort, provides activities including shopping, parking, hotel accommodation, entertainment, and religious worship.

The second is located on the waterfront and is accessible mainly by water transport. It contains an aquarium, marina, luxury accommodations, and convention facilities, as well as beach access to the Red Sea.

The Vancouver firm of Aitken Wreglesworth Associates, Architects Ltd., in collaboration with Arthur Erickson, was commissioned to design these two zones. As part of the resulting design presentation, a 15-minute marketing video was produced. The video included 4.5 minutes of computer animation, which was provided by E.V. Radvenis Inc.; this took five months to complete.

PROJECT
Interior view of a
Show Piece pulp mill
control room
Kalimantan Timur,
Indonesia

CLIENT
H.A. Simons Ltd.
Vancouver, B.C.

ARCHITECTURAL ILLUSTRATION
828 CHARLES ALLEN DRIVE, N.E.
ATLANTA, GEORGIA 30308
404-876-3943
404-876-3943 FAX

PROJECT
Bangkok Dome
Retail Facility (Exterior)

ARCHITECT
FRCH Worldwide

RENDERING SIZE
14" x 16" (36 cm x 41 cm)

MEDIUM
Ink, watercolor

PROJECT
Bangkok Dome
Retail Facility (Interior)

ARCHITECT
FRCH Worldwide

RENDERING SIZE
12" x 15" (30 cm x 38 cm)

MEDIUM
Ink, watercolor

Barbara Worth Ratner, AIA

Barbara Worth Ratner has recognized that offering a wide and flexible range of illustration techniques and services enables her to grasp her clients' specific needs as opportunities to work with thoughtful client-collaborators to find artistically successful, realistic, and often unique solutions to each situation. The positive results of the breadth of Ratner's effort to meet diverse needs are well reflected in her exhibited works. In a group of seven of the prestigious annual Architecture in Perspective exhibitions, Ratner was represented by works in each of five media: watercolor (currently her primary medium), acrylics, ink, colored pencil, and cut Pantone film.

Along with this portfolio of techniques, Ratner brings a special emphasis on the presentation of human figures within architectural settings. As a result, she has been frequently commissioned for retail and recreational projects, including a long series of venue illustrations in connection with the 1996 and 2004 Summer Olympic Games. Ratner's studio is equipped for computer generation of perspective layouts. In several successful experiments, she has worked closely with computer-reliant designers and associates to produce final images generated jointly by handwork and by computer.

PROJECT
Oxford College Housing
Emory University at Oxford, Georgia

CLIENT
Lord, Aeck & Sargent

RENDERING SIZE
19" x 12" (48 cm x 30 cm)

MEDIUM
Watercolor

PROJECT
Centennial Olympic Park
Atlanta, Georgia
LANDSCAPE ARCHITECTS
EDAW Inc.
RENDERING SIZE
16" x 10" (41 cm x 25 cm)
MEDIUM
Watercolor

INSET IMAGES:
(Clockwise from upper left)
PROJECT
Centennial Olympic Park
RENDERING SIZE
(two views)
16" x 11" (41 cm x 25 cm)
MEDIUM
Watercolor

PROJECT
Olympic Tennis Venue
Stone Mountain, Georgia
CLIENT
Nichols Carter Grant,
Architects
RENDERING SIZE
12" x 20" (30 cm x 51 cm)
MEDIUM
Watercolor

PROJECT
Proposed Volleyball Venue
at Cobb County Galleria
CLIENT
Smallwood, Reynolds,
Stewart, Stewart, and
Associates Inc.
RENDERING SIZE
8" x 11" (20 cm x 28 cm)
MEDIUM
Prismacolor pencil

PROJECT
Proposed Gymnastics Venue
Atlanta Committee for the
Olympic Games
RENDERING SIZE
5" x 9" (13 cm x 23 cm)
MEDIUM
Prismacolor pencil

PROJECT
Georgia International Horse
Park Equestrian Venue
CLIENT
Lord, Aeck & Sargent
RENDERING SIZE
(two views adjoining
Gymnastics)
16" x 10" (41 cm x 25 cm)
MEDIUM
Watercolor

168 *Barbara Worth Ratner*

PROJECT
McDuffie Satellite Center,
Voc-Tech School
Thomson, Georgia

CLIENT
Lord, Aeck & Sargent

RENDERING SIZE
5" x 6" (13 cm x 15 cm)

MEDIUM
Watercolor

HONORABLE MENTION
Architecture in
Perspective 10

PROJECT
Manufacturing Related
Disciplines Complex
Georgia Institute of Technology

CLIENT
Lord, Aeck & Sargent

RENDERING SIZE
28" x 8" (71 cm x 20 cm)

MEDIUM
Watercolor on computer-
generated line drawing

EXHIBITED
Architecture in Perspective II

PROJECT
Scholars' Press
Atlanta, Georgia

CLIENT
Lord, Aeck & Sargent

RENDERING SIZE
5" x 6" (13 cm x 15 cm)

MEDIUM
Watercolor

EXHIBITED
A Perspectivists' Salon
New York School of
Interior Design

CLIENT LIST

Lord, Aeck & Sargent

EDAW

Nichols Carter Grant

*Atlanta Committee for the
Olympic Games*

*Commission for the 2004
Olympiad (San Juan)*

*Marvel Flores Cobian &
Asociados*

Diedrich and Associates

Emory University

Boston College

Altamira

Sizemore Floyd

Smith Dalia

Heery International

*Thompson, Ventulett,
Stainback, and Associates*

Cooper Carry and Associates

Roberts & Collins

Simons-Eastern

Turner Associates

Kell Muñoz Wigodsky

Stang & Newdow

Rosser Fabrap International

PROJECT
Robert C. Goizueta Building
School of Business Administration
Emory University, Atlanta, Georgia

CLIENT
Kallmann, McKinnell, and Wood

RENDERING SIZE
19" x 15" (48 cm x 38 cm)

MEDIUM
Watercolor

PROJECT
Ichauway Administration

CLIENT
Lord, Aeck & Sargent

RENDERING SIZE
16" x 7" (41 cm x 18 cm)

MEDIUM
Watercolor

PROJECT
Plaza Indonesia Retail
Facility

CLIENT
FRCH Worldwide

RENDERING SIZE
9" x 20" (23 cm x 51 cm)

MEDIUM
Felt-tip pen, watercolor

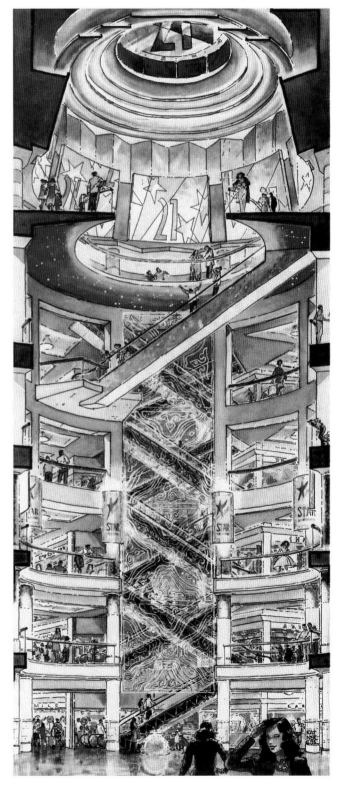

5433 BOYD AVENUE
OAKLAND, CALIFORNIA 94618
510-655-7030 (PHONE AND FAX)

PROJECT
Capitol Mall Competition
Sacramento, California

CLIENT
Skidmore Owings and Merrill

RENDERING SIZE
14" x 18" (36 cm x 46 cm)

MEDIUM
Charcoal and color pencil

PROJECT
KFIC Tower, Seoul, Korea

CLIENT
James Stewart Polshek
and Partners

RENDERING SIZE
18" x 25" (46 cm x 64 cm)

MEDIUM
Watercolor

Michael Reardon

Since 1979, Michael Reardon has provided a variety of illustration services in North America and abroad. Styles range from atmospheric sketches to fully articulated illustrations.

Reardon believes that the most dynamic illustrations result from active collaboration between the artist and client. Every effort is made to interpret the client's vision into the most interesting image possible.

PROJECT
Martin Luther King, Jr. Plaza

CLIENT
Charles Dickey (original)
IDG Group (renovation)

RENDERING SIZE
12" x 22" (31 cm x 56 cm)

MEDIUM
Watercolor

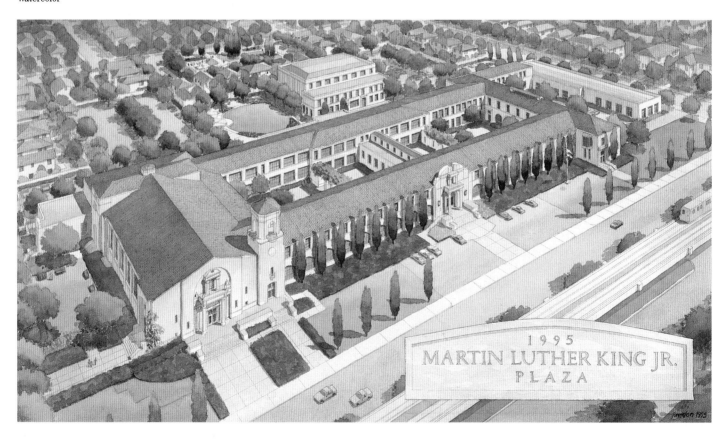

PROJECT
Bangkok International Airport
Bangkok, Thailand

CLIENT
Hellmuth Obata Kassabaum, Inc.

RENDERING SIZE
10" x 14" (25 cm x 36 cm)

MEDIUM
Color pencil

PROJECT
Napa Valley Residence
Napa, California

CLIENT
Backen, Arrigoni & Ross

RENDERING SIZE
8" x 11" (20 cm x 28 cm)

MEDIUM
Color pencil

PROJECT
Mobile Casino,
Mobile, Alabama

CLIENT
Projects International

RENDERING SIZE
8" x 11" (20 cm x 28 cm)

MEDIUM
Color pencil

PROJECT
Mobile Casino
Mobile, Alabama

CLIENT
Projects International

RENDERING SIZE
8" x 11" (20 cm x 28 cm)

MEDIUM
Color pencil

PROJECT
Cinema Walk Elevation
Toyko, Japan

CLIENT
Projects International

RENDERING SIZE
8" x 10" (20 cm x 25 cm)

MEDIUM
Color pencil

Michael Reardon   175

PROJECT
Interlochen Center for the Arts
Interlochen, Michigan

CLIENT
Sasaki Associates

RENDERING SIZE
12" x 24" (31 cm x 61 cm)

MEDIUM
Watercolor

PROJECT
Taman Dayu Resort
Indonesia

CLIENT
Projects International

RENDERING SIZE
14" x 22" (36 cm x 56 cm)

MEDIUM
Watercolor

PROJECT
Taman Dayu Resort
Indonesia

CLIENT
Projects International

RENDERING SIZE
14" x 22" (36 cm x 56 cm)

MEDIUM
Watercolor

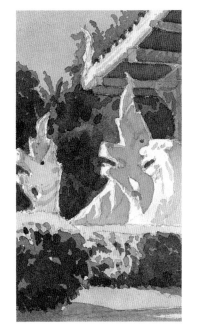

PROJECT
Travel Sketches
RENDERING SIZE
4" X 7" (10 cm x 17.5 cm)
MEDIUM
Watercolor

PROJECT
"Jason and the Betternots"
Book Illustration
RENDERING SIZE
5" x 10" (13 cm x 25 cm)
MEDIUM
Watercolor

ROCHON ASSOCIATES, INC.
13530 MICHIGAN AVENUE, SUITE 205
DEARBORN, MICHIGAN 48126
313-584-9580
313-584-4071 FAX

Richard Rochon

Entering his 35th year as a delineator, Richard Rochon continues to meet the expectations of an international clientele. With attention to detail, Rochon incorporates atmospheric drama and realism to convey the unique character of each project. This has been the basis of success for Rochon Associates, Inc. Through the collaborative efforts of the staff at Rochon Associates, client relations have been developed and strengthened by maintaining a consistently high standard of comprehensive service and timely delivery.

PROFESSIONAL AFFILIATIONS

Honorary Member,
Michigan Society of Architects

Advisory Council, College of Architecture and
Design, Lawrence Technological University

Author, Color in Architectural Illustration
(Van Nostrand Reinhold, 1989)

Regional Coordinator, American Society of
Architectural Perspectivists

CLIENT LIST

Arquitectonica, Coral Gables, Florida

Gunnar Birkerts, Birmingham, Michigan

Cambridge Seven Associates,
Cambridge, Massachusetts

Hellmuth Obata Kassabaum, New York,
New York; Shanghai, China; St. Louis,
Missouri; Washington, District of
Columbia

Lohan Associates, Chicago, Illinois

Nikken Sekkei, Tokyo, Japan

Pei-Cobb-Freed & Partners, New York,
New York

Rossetti Associates, Birmingham,
Michigan; Santa Monica, California

Skidmore, Owings & Merrill, Chicago,
Illinois; London, England; New York,
New York; Washington, District of
Columbia

Smith, Hinchamn & Grylls Associates,
Detroit, Michigan

2112 Broadway #407
New York, New York 10023
212-362-5524
212-362-5719 FAX

PROJECT
Friedrichstadt Passagen
Berlin, Germany

ARCHITECT
Pei Cobb Freed and
Partners

RENDERING SIZE
18" x 24" (46 cm x 61 cm)

MEDIUM
Watercolor

Thomas Wells Schaller, AIA

"When building strives to become more than mere shelter, architecture, and an architectural presence, is born. And when drawing attempts to convey both the tangible and the more subjective qualities of this presence, architectural artwork is created."

For the past 12 years, the work of Thomas Schaller, registered architect and architectural artist, has provided a study in the attempt to understand and to capture, in two-dimensional form, this elusive presence. Schaller's work has—through innumerable exhibits, publications, lectures, and a thriving international practice—become respected worldwide. Schaller writes that the profession of the architectural artist is unique in its attempt to visually interpret the nonexistent material body. The most successful examples of architectural artwork must often simultaneously possess the organizational lucidity of the orthagonal design document, the pictorial approachability of the topographical landscape painting, and the scope, reach, and grace of visionary art."

PROJECT
Friedrichstadt Passagen
Berlin, Germany

CLIENT
Pei Cobb Freed & Partners

RENDERING SIZE
18" x 24" (46 cm x 61 cm)

MEDIUM
Watercolor

PROJECT
Untitled

ARCHITECT
Thomas W. Schaller, AIA

RENDERING SIZE
24" x 18" (61 cm x 46 cm)

MEDIUM
Watercolor

E CITY COULD BE MADE IN THE IMAGE OF MA

PROJECT
California Civic Center Competition
San Franciso

CLIENT
Kohn Pedersen Fox Associates, P.C.

RENDERING SIZE
12" x 12" (31 cm x 31 cm)

MEDIUM
Pencil and watercolor

PROJECT
Baltimore Performing Arts
Center Competition Proposal

CLIENT
Lett/Smith Architects, Toronto

RENDERING SIZE
24" x 18" (61 cm x 46 cm)

MEDIUM
Watercolor

PROJECT
Proposed Development

CLIENT
Aldo Rossi: Studio di
Architettura

RENDERING SIZE
11" x 17" (28 cm x 43 cm)

MEDIUM
Watercolor

PROJECT
Orpheus in Orlando

ARCHITECT
Thomas W. Schaller, AIA

RENDERING SIZE
22" x 30" (56 cm x 76 cm)

MEDIUM
Watercolor

PROJECT
Life Magazine Dream House

ARCHITECT
Dennis W. Wedlick,
Architect

CLIENT
Life Magazine

RENDERING SIZE
18" x 24" (46 cm x 61 cm)

MEDIUM
Watercolor

PROJECT
Dulles Airport Concourse
Washington, D.C.

CLIENT
Hellmuth Obata &
Kassabaum

RENDERING SIZE
24" x 24" (61 cm x 61 cm)

MEDIUM
Watercolor

PROJECT
Proposed Hydroponics
Research Center, Uruguay

ARCHITECT
Thomas W. Schaller, AIA

RENDERING SIZE
24" x 18" (61 cm x 46 cm)

MEDIUM
Watercolor

PROJECT
House, Naples, Florida

CLIENT
Richard Meier & Partners

RENDERING SIZE
18" x 24" (46 cm x 61 cm)

MEDIUM
Watercolor

*President Emeritus–Advisory Council–
The American Society of Architectural
Perspectivists*

*Fellow–The Society of Architectural and
Industrial Illustrators/Great Britain*

*Member–The New York Society
of Renderers*

*The Hugh Ferriss Memorial Prize–
Architecture in Perspective III; 1988*

*Formal Presentation Award–
Architecture in Perspective VIII; 1993*

*Formal Presentation Award–
Architecture in Perspective IX; 1994*

*Juror's Award–Architecture in
Perspective VI; 1991*

*Honor Awards–Architecture in
Perspective I, II, III, IV, V, VI, VII,
VIII, IX, X, XI; 1986–1996*

*Author–*Architecture in Watercolor,
Van Nostrand Reinhold: 1990

*Author–*Images of Architecture,
Van Nostrand Reinhold: 1996

*Citation for Excellence–Architecture
in Watercolor; 1991 AIA International
Book Awards*

PROJECT
La Defense Development
Proposal, Paris
CLIENT
Cesar Pelli & Associates
RENDERING SIZE
11" x 17" (28 cm x 43 cm)
MEDIUM
Pencil, watercolor

PROJECT
J.F.K. International Airport
Competition
CLIENT
Kohn Pedersen Fox Associates, P.C.
RENDERING SIZE
18" x 18" (46 cm x 46 cm)
MEDIUM
Pencil

PROJECT
Resort Proposal, Portugal
CLIENT
Arquitectonica
RENDERING SIZE
11" x 17" (28 cm x 43 cm)
MEDIUM
Watercolor

PROJECT
Proposed Telecom-
munications Tower
Jakarta, Indonesia

CLIENT
Skidmore Owings & Merrill

RENDERING SIZE
17" x 11" (43 cm x 28 cm)

MEDIUM
Pencil, watercolor

CLIENT LIST

Kohn Pedersen Fox Associates, P.C.
Skidmore Owings & Merrill
Pei Cobb Freed & Partners
Cesar Pelli & Associates
James Stewart Polshek & Partners
Perkins & Will
Hellmuth, Obata & Kassabaum
Cooper Robertson & Partners
Mitchell/Giurgola Architects
Gwathmey Siegel & Associates
Aldo Rossi—Studio di Architettura
Richard Meier & Partners
Venturi, Scott Brown & Associates;
Anderson/Swartz Architects
Raphael Vignoly Architects
Beyer Blinder Belle
Hardy Holzman Pfeiffer Associates
Nikken Sekkei Ltd.
Ellerbe Becket
RTKL

PROJECT
Proposed Planetarium
New York, New York

CLIENT
James Stewart Polshek
and Partners

RENDERING SIZE
11" x 17" (28 cm x 43 cm)

MEDIUM
Watercolor

PROJECT
Proposed Corporate
Headquarters
Armonk, New York

CLIENT
Kohn Pedersen Fox
Associates, P.C.

RENDERING SIZE
11" x 17" (28 cm x 43 cm)

MEDIUM
Pencil, watercolor

The Creative Dilemma

By Frank M. Costantino, asap, fsai, jara

Strongly committed as illustrators remain to their profession, the rationale behind their work has become increasingly important. The inscrutable, always challenging thought process for creating an architectural image is as intriguing and exciting as the execution of the building itself. Without formal art training, some practitioners have had to acquire the confidence to make visual judgments from design principles adapted from an architectural training. They also rely on the works of the masters to secure a grasp of the elusive energy that gives drawing its powers.

My definition of this dynamic of drawing might read this way: "a fluid, emergent process whereby an image defines itself as technique is applied to paper." The development of an architectural perspective is influenced by personal and professional experience, the comforting prejudice of previous successes and client expectations, and the unsettling tension of aesthetic response to many visual criteria. All of this embodies the creative struggle between objective response to an architect's hard data of design drawings and subjective interpretation of a projected reality.

Hugh Ferriss wrote in the 1929 edition of *Encyclopedia Britannica* that rendering has six objectives:

> ... the first three have long been recognized: to convey advance realizations of proposed structures, to aid in crystallizing ideas in the architect's mind and to *interpret the significance* of existing structures. The other three remain largely for future development: to serve as [a] criterion and guide in city planning, to assist in evolving new types of architecture and to strengthen the psychological influence of architecture on human values...

Anyone seeking to attain some mastery of their work would likely be well enough engaged in the first three objectives, and letting the value of the remaining three be left to the vagaries of time or the subject of another discourse. My fascination with the dynamic of the second and third of these points has become a central point in my process.

DISCOVERY AND EVALUATION

As the talent of architectural illustrators evolves over time, their sensitivities toward the subtler aspects of drawing and the possibilities of interpretation likewise expand. In discovering that a broader array of visual choices are available for effectively devising an image of an architect's design, two scenarios dominate: a more deliberate structuring of the multiple elements that comprise perspective images, their thoughtful development, and their skillful execution on schedule; and in situations such as competitions —a similar, but much swifter, responsive process to the demands of an extremely condensed time frame.

With the experience of producing drawings and successfully dealing with architect and owner in their different languages, the illustrator can enjoy the luxury of investigating a wide spectrum of drawing options that would allow for an informative, descriptive image, at the least; and if the inspiration so directs, a visually powerful rendition emulating the work of this profession's masters. However, the triad of efforts between architect, illustrator, and the client/owner invariably tend to focus on different aspects of the building, and for the interim period when the perspective plays a fairly crucial role in the design process, a visual synthesis delicately balances the architect's aesthetics with the client's needs for a promotional tool.

The illustrator's artistic process can be characterized as a channel, a linear sequence of technical development for producing the work. The difference between a competent descriptive drawing and one that is arresting and beautiful lies in the random, curvilinear impulses that can infuse great impact. Observation of these impulses is what remains most intriguing to me, and, from discussions with my masterful colleagues, to them as well.

Aware of the working of these impulses, and inspired by predecessors such as Jules Guerin, Hugh Ferriss, Cyril Farey, Samuel Chamberlain, and fine artists like Homer, Sargent, Canaletto and Hopper, it seems to me that every commission presents numerous possibilities for interpreting the design of the architect. There could be little argument that Ferriss's image of the Chrysler Building presents a unique vision of the structure as memorable as architect William Van Alen's original inspiration, or even one's own impressions from visits to the structure. The primary emphasis in Ferriss's drawing was "an impression of the extreme dimensions" of the structure, then the tallest building in the world, and the resultant undelineated facades and massive vagueness of the surrounding context of mid-Manhattan. It is Ferriss's legacy of poetic imagery that not only influenced the architecture of the '20s, '30s and '40s, but remains the enduring standard of excellence for that era. In another approach, the exquisitely crafted image of New York's Ford Foundation building by Helmut Jacoby remains as engaging a representation of Roche Dinkeloo's creation as the elegant building itself still presents on Fifth Avenue. Jacoby's unique pen-and-ink, shaded style of illustration—derived and adapted from the Beaux Arts tradition—creates informative elegance with its extremely precise rendition, which incorporates every architectural detail in the building. Jacoby's work remains the benchmark of illustration for the '60s and '70s.

Such artistry embodies the phenomenon of aesthetics; its unquestionable impact can provide inspiration to the contemporary illustrator for achieving similar ends. Basing my view of the struggle for artistic expression on the fact that the architectural illustrator should, ideally, be trained in architecture and, perhaps, the fine arts, I feel that aesthetic concerns should extend beyond a building's design elements alone, addressing in addition the abstract characteristics of light, space, time, volume, and texture. These characteristics are existential concepts that imbue the innumerable features of architecture and can be reinterpreted into a driving rationale for producing a strong representation of the design. The method for deciding on a specific approach, assuming the existence of the technical capability to realize it, introduces a host of other factors, a few of which can be addressed in the remaining paragraphs.

THE IMPORTANCE OF INTENT

During the initial stages of an illustration project, the design material provided by the architect outlines a building's form and usually includes the plan, elevation, section, site, detail drawings, and, sometimes, context photos. These documents form the basis from which the illustrator may consider a reasonably descriptive view or two, or even three; the number of views can make a decided difference in how to represent the subject. Depending on when the illustrator is introduced to the project, there may be material colors provided, and maybe even "wireframe" computer views.

Basic, two-dimensional data form the groundwork on which the perspective artist constructs a three-dimensional view. The visual acuity of a perspectivist is such that a well-proportioned, three-dimensional sketch can be easily drawn without instruments, and certainly becomes the starting point of thought for the work. This fact continues to be the case despite the recent explosion of computer 3-D modeling and rendering capabilities, which can inform architects at nearly every level of practice in the modeling of their designs and have otherwise supplanted the hand-drawn perspective sketches of traditionally trained architects. However informative the measured design sketches and computer drawings may be, they only suggest depth, texture, light, color, and many other attributes that become the principal concerns of the illustrator, who will use them to enliven the architecture and provide it with its intended beauty. In effectively realizing the vision of the architect, who is wrestling with the same concerns, the illustrator may bring a refreshing (sometimes eye-opening) viewpoint, achieving a more tangible representation. These concerns serve as the reference dialogue between illustrator and architect to derive some mutual drawing directives.

The perspectivist, as a temporary consultant in a rather extended process, at best generates a visual interpretation that may result in a favorable image of the proposed project, the impact of which may survive the artist's limited involvement. As discussed earlier, interpretation combines the perspectivist's media skills, personal visual experience, architectural sensitivities, and an intuitive response to the spatial character of the building and its site. Therein lies the array of choices for selecting media, determining the method of its application, evaluating the building's features, and perhaps setting a focus on a major element, planning a harmonious composition, choosing the time of day (or night), and its related atmosphere: these are all valid considerations for solving the visual problem of a perspective. For example, watercolor can be employed in a tightly controlled fashion to depict the steel, glass, and monochromatic materials of an office building; whereas, a slick paper and soft pencil could be used in a very smooth tonal technique for the same building. Possibly, a certain contrast to the architecture can be provided by a very disciplined watercolor handling of the subject building combined with a looser suggestion of the context.

Given the technical nature of the field, certain constraints for proportion, accuracy, and definition do have to be assumed as necessary to the final result. The measured delineation, however, does not dictate that all line work must be precisely articulated with straight-edge instruments. Since computer imagery has now reached such sophisticated levels of modeling, it may be preferable for the artist to intentionally avoid such precision; a choice for a freehand line may imbue a very desirable quality to the architecture by virtue of edge softness. A much more interpretive handling might better serve the architect if the uses for an image are initially investigative of certain design qualities and are intended for limited view. The "fuzzy" phases of conceptual or schematic design drawings, for example, quite often offer a wider latitude for the illustrator's influence, simply because many detail decisions

cannot be made so early. The design may be required for a competition that limits development with a rigid time frame. For this purpose, a more fluid technique of drawing or painting would more admirably represent the design, while perhaps saying more with what is not conveyed, leaving a little to the viewer's imagination, thereby underscoring a design's worthiness for solving the problem and convincing a jury.

Such fluidity seemed to be the way the great English artist, William Walcot, responded to his commissions. Sir Edwin Lutyens, in describing Walcot's visits to his office, remarked that "...when he was going to do a perspective, he would come into the office and quietly wander around for a couple of days. You'd look up and find him watching over your shoulder as you were drawing. Then he would go away and later produce a wonderful watercolor in his own distinctive style." Walcot attuned himself to the architect's thinking and responded in a fashion that was both descriptive of what he observed and expressive of his own understanding. In doing so, he acknowledged the inspired response by commenting, "I feel it with my brush; I don't draw it."

Thus, the choices for depicting the architecture become a critical matter. They may be made narrower by the factors of budget, time, drawing size, skill level, and architect or client preferences. Nonetheless, a versatile illustrator should be flexible enough to select methods that best interpret the design and still achieve a visually effective image.

THE EXPRESSIVE EXECUTION; DIDACTIC VS. INSPIRATIONAL WORK

In drawing buildings, the perspectivist confronts the difficulty of generating a single image to convey substance and impart a reality of environment. Each illustration is a commercial enterprise: one's services will enhance the value of the architect's design and the client/owner's interest in realizing a successful project.

In addressing not only the architect's sense of the building, but also the client's promotional needs for the perspective, the illustrator's attempts to merge the efforts of the highly trained architect with the client's less-refined—but otherwise intuitive—sense to devise a drawing that will best serve the project. The illustration is also a symbolic work that stands as testimony to the efforts of many people. To the degree that the illustrator's work achieves a visual power and an aesthetic quality, it will create a tangible image which furthers the interests of satisfied parties who pay the commission, and helps to provide financing for a project.

Realizing the power of buildings in an illustration is the goal of artistic intent. By recognizing the unique, multi-level problems that the work of drawing must resolve, the renderer wrestles in realms of artistic decisions with the discretion of informed experiences to delicately handle subtle relationships of value, color, and line in a certain choice of media. Empowered by an aesthetic premise, the illustrator ideally will combine these many drawing choices to produce an engaging image that overpowers the viewer, stimulates the imagination, conveys excitement, and describes the design completely.

On this point, Hugh Ferriss, regarded as "the philosopher" of his profession, said that "to portray the building is to portray something that does not exist; rendering is an exercise in imagination.... [it] must be fully controlled by a realization of the structural facts involved. It is a matter of equating artistic reach to architectural grasp." Given the variables for expression, the dynamics of this equation can be considerably complex.

Ultimately, to make convincing architectural images is the real work of the perspectivist. The interpretive skill of combining design information with media choices into a focused intent provides the tension for expression. An interesting notion comes from Lawrence Wright, author of *Perspective On Perspective*, who writes that the perspector's "function is only interpretive, but so are those of the actor, the singer, the conductor and orchestra," and their achievements are frequently "artistic," although in comparison, they are ephemeral.

A RESOLUTION

Illustrators must critically assess the strength of their skills by comparing their own current and earlier work, as well as with that of our predecessors, and must develop flexibility of expression through continued study and practice. To feel moved by the works of Otto Wagner, Frank Lloyd Wright or Charles Rennie Mackintosh suggests that, by adapting some aspect of their technique, further insight into their thinking may be achieved. The exquisite compositions of Cyril Farey, the delicate portrayals of David Roberts, and the remarkable imagery of Hiroshige teach unspoken lessons. Farey, the preeminent British watercolorist whose resurgent influence is evident today, blended the Beaux Arts methods with a British style of drawing whereby a combined precision with a delicate, imaginative use of color conveyed a "romantic aura" upon the buildings he painted.

The influence of fine art imagery should tighten the fabric of the aesthetic—existential—sense and dress the necessary technical—didactic—skills in a costume of elegance. The finer matter of the illustrator's efforts is attaining that artistic level of an arresting visual message. That worthy goal must still be sought in the composition and color studies of a drawing; in the color palette choices of pencil, watercolor, airbrush or other medium; in the texture of vellum, paper, film, mylar, or even canvas. A fluid drawing process for combining these elements, applied in an economy of means with an economy of experience, will assist the image in magically manifesting itself before the eyes. With mastery comes facility; with facility comes freshness; with freshness comes a vigor of statement. A flow derives from the confident response to the aesthetic tensions. Therein lies the excitement, pleasure, and satisfaction of the architectural drawing.

SHIRAI PERS HOUSE
31-8-213 HONCHO,
WAKO-SHI, SAITAMA-KEN
351-01 JAPAN
048-465-1615 (PHONE AND FAX)

PROJECT
Innoshima Bridge
Hiroshima, Japan

CLIENT
Honshu-Shikoku Bridge Authority
Hiroshima-ken, Japan

RENDERING SIZE
17" x 12" (42 cm x 30 cm)

MEDIUM
Airbrush, pen and ink

PROJECT
Nakanosakaue Project
Tokyo, Japan

CLIENT
Helm Archiship, Yamamoto
Hori Architects, Tokyo, Japan

RENDERING SIZE
24" x 17" (59 cm x 42 cm)

MEDIUM
Airbrush, pen and ink

Hideo Shirai

PROJECT
Nakanosakaue Project
Tokyo, Japan

CLIENT
Helm Archiship
Nihon Sekkei Inc.
Institute of New Architecture
Tokyo, Japan

RENDERING SIZE
24" x 17" (59 cm x 42 cm)

MEDIUM
Airbrush, pen and ink

PROJECT
Yokohama International Port Terminal
Design Competition
Yokohama, Japan

CLIENT
Helm Archiship, Tokyo, Japan

RENDERING SIZE
17" x 14" (42 cm x 36 cm)

MEDIUM
Airbrush, pen and ink

PROJECT
Dream

CLIENT
Hideo Shirai

RENDERING SIZE
24" x 17" (59 cm x 42 cm)

MEDIUM
Airbrush, pen and ink

PROJECT
Tokyo Metropolitan Subway
National Stadium Station
Tokyo, Japan

CLIENT
Yoichiro Hosaka Architect and Associates
Tokyo, Japan

RENDERING SIZE
29" x 15" (72 cm x 38 cm)

MEDIUM
Airbrush, pen and ink

PROJECT
Maison de la Culture
du Japon à Paris
Paris, France

CLIENT
Taisei Corp. Design and
Proposal Division
Tokyo, Japan

RENDERING SIZE
17" x 12" (42 cm x 30 cm)

MEDIUM
Airbrush, pen and ink

PROJECT
Yaesu Project
Tokyo, Japan

CLIENT
Shigeru Shindo
A & T Associates
Tokyo, Japan

RENDERING SIZE
24" x 17" (59 cm x 42 cm)

MEDIUM
Airbrush, pen and ink

PROJECT
Sapporo Community Dome
Sapporo, Japan

CLIENT
Mitsubishi Estate Co. Ltd.
Atelier Bnk Co. Ltd.
Taisei Corp./Sapporo City,
Tokyo and Sapporo, Japan

RENDERING SIZE
14" x 20" (72 cm x 50 cm)

MEDIUM
Airbrush, pen and ink

PROJECT (BOTH)
Oriental Concert Hall, China
CLIENT
Nihon Sekkei Inc., Tokyo, Japan
RENDERING SIZE
29" x 20" (72 cm x 51 cm)
MEDIUM
Airbrush, pen and ink

PROJECT
Natori Performing Arts Center, Miyagi, Japan
CLIENT
Fumihiko Maki, Tokyo, Japan
RENDERING SIZE
24" x 16" (61 cm x 40 cm)
MEDIUM
Pen, airbrush, and watercolor

PROJECT
Chiba Floral Museum
Chiba-shi, Japan

CLIENT
Shigeru Shindo, A & T Associates
Tokyo, Japan

RENDERING SIZE
24" x 17" (59 cm x 42 cm)

MEDIUM
Airbrush, pen and ink

Hideo Shirai   199

RAEL D. SLUTSKY & ASSOCIATES, INC.
ARCHITECTURAL IMAGING
351 MILFORD ROAD
DEERFIELD, ILLINOIS 60015

PROJECT
Lyric Opera of Chicago Expansion
Chicago, Illinois

CLIENT
Skidmore, Owings & Merrill
Chicago, Illinois

RENDERING SIZE
10" x 16" (25 cm x 41 cm)

MEDIUM
Freehand pen & ink,
color pencil

Rael D. Slutsky, AIA

Internationally renowned for fine pen-and-ink renderings, Rael D. Slutsky & Associates is a responsive, creative and professional source for architectural imaging. The firm provides comprehensive services to a diverse, distinguished clientele with a range of rendering techniques from freehand sketching to computer-generated 3-D animation. Mr. Slutsky's work has been exhibited widely at galleries and museums in the Unites States and Canada, as well as in Europe, South America, and the Far East; numerous books and periodicals have published his work.

Slutsky's work distinguishes itself by an unparalleled combination of dramatic impact and uncompromising detail that results from his process of thorough view-analysis, extensive studies and constant experimentation. Each project is invested with a uniquely individual character and the highest quality imagery using a variety of media. Most of the firm's drawing techniques yield both black-and-white and color versions of each original rendering.

The firm has been honored with thirteen awards—including the 1994 Hugh Ferriss Memorial Prize—from the annual international "Architecture In Perspective" competition, sponsored by the American Society of Architectural Perspectivists (ASAP). Mr. Slutsky is a past President and currently Advisory Counselor for ASAP; he also served as officer of the Newhouse Architecture Foundation in Chicago and holds membership in the American Institute of Architects.

PROJECT
Orchestra Hall—New Additions
Chicago, Illinois

CLIENT
Skidmore, Owings & Merrill
Chicago, Illinois

RENDERING SIZE
18" x 24" (46 cm x 61 cm)

MEDIUM
Freehand pen & ink,
color pencil and pastel

Hugh Ferriss Memorial Prize—
1994 Architecture in Perspective 9 Competition

PROJECT
Third Government Center Competition
Daejeon, Korea

CLIENT
Kunwon International, Seoul, Korea

RENDERING SIZE
30" x 40" (76 cm x 102 cm)

MEDIUM
Formal pen & ink, color pencil, and pastel

"The image, a bold and vigorous inktone and color drawing for an urban government center competition in Korea, has an overall sense of spontaneity and a wondrous gestural quality that epitomizes Rael Slutsky's much honored body of work. In describing Slutsky's award-winning entry, AIP 9 juror Ronald Love observed, "I felt that this year's Hugh Ferriss Award winner, like previous winners, reached beyond the usual commonplace image to a higher plane of artistic achievement. The bold, poster-like quality and the dynamic use of a limited color palette, along with the strong contrasts of light and dark, gave it a sense of power and mystery."

— Jury Comments, *Architecture in Perspective 9*

OTHER AWARDS

Juror's Award—Architecture in Perspective 4

Best of Sketch Category Award—Architecture in Perspective 7

9 Honor Awards-Architecture in Perspective 2, 3, 6, 8, 9

CLIENT LIST

A. Epstein & Sons, International
Altoon & Porter
Cesar Pelli & Associates
Dong Bu Consulting (Seoul)
FM Associates
Hellmuth Obata & Kassabaum
Holabird & Root
Homart Development
Kunwon Associates (Seoul)
Lohan Associates
McCann Erickson (Zurich, New York)

Murphy/Jahn
Nikken Sekkei (Osaka)
O'Donnell, Wicklund, Pegozzi & Peterson
Pei Cobb Freed & Partners
Perkins & Will
RTKL
Skidmore, Owings & Merrill
Schal/Bovis
Stein & Company

PROJECT
One Liberty Place
Philadelphia, Pennsylvania

CLIENT
Murphy/Jahn, Chicago, Illinois

RENDERING SIZE
18" x 28" (46 cm x 71 cm)

MEDIUM
Formal pen & ink, color pencil,
and airbrush

PROJECT
Southeast Financial Center
Tampa, Florida

CLIENT
Cooper Cary
Atlanta, Georgia

RENDERING SIZE
11" x 16" (28 cm x 41 cm)

MEDIUM
Formal pen & ink, color pencil

PROJECT
Parks at Arlington Mall
Arlington, Texas

CLIENT
F/M Associates
Dallas, Texas

RENDERING SIZE
12" x 24" (31 cm x 61 cm)

MEDIUM
Formal felt tip pen and
color pencil

PROJECT
Lyric Opera of Chicago Expansion,
Chicago, Illinois

CLIENT
Skidmore, Owings & Merrill,
Chicago, Illinois

RENDERING SIZE
10" x 16" (25 cm x 41 cm)

MEDIUM
Freehand pen & ink, color pencil

PROJECT
East Bank Waterfront Towers
Grand Rapids, Michigan

CLIENT
A. Epstein & Sons International

RENDERING SIZE
14" x 26" (36 cm x 66 cm)

MEDIUM
Formal pen & ink,
color pencil, and pastel

PROJECT
Bishopgate 9/10 Building, London, England

CLIENT
Skidmore, Owings & Merrill

RENDERING SIZE
18" x 24" (46 cm x 61 cm)

MEDIUM
Formal pen & ink, color pencil, and airbrush

PROJECT
The Point Townhomes, Chicago, Illinois

CLIENT
Roy Hl. Kruse & Associates

RENDERING SIZE
10" x 16" (25 cm x 41 cm)

MEDIUM
Freehand pen & ink, color pencil, and pastel

PROJECT
Seoul Electronic Exchange
Seoul, Korea

CLIENT
Skidmore, Owings & Merrill
Chicago, Illinois

RENDERING SIZE
15" x 15" (38 cm x 38 cm)

MEDIUM
Formal pen & ink,
color pencil and pastel

PROJECT
Egandale Townhomes
Chicago, Illinois

CLIENT
David Swan
Chicago, Illinois

RENDERING SIZE
10" x 16" (25 cm x 41 cm)

MEDIUM
Freehand felt tip pen
and color pencil

PROJECT
Master Plan Project

RENDERING SIZE
8" x 10" (20 cm x 25 cm)

MEDIUM
Freehand felt tip pen, color
pencil, and pastel

PROJECT
Republic Bank
Dallas, Texas

CLIENT
Skidmore, Owings & Merrill

RENDERING SIZE
12" x 12" (30 cm x 30 cm)

MEDIUM
Freehand felt tip pen
and color pencil

PROJECT
National Bank of Poland
Warsaw, Poland

CLIENT
Kohn Perdersen Fox Associates
New York, New York

A. Epstein & Sons International
Chicago, Illinois

RENDERING SIZE
8.5" x 11" (22 cm x 28 cm)

MEDIUM
Freehand felt tip, pastel, and color pencil

PROJECT
New Oasis Resort
Michigan City, Michigan

CLIENT
Chicago Consultants Group
Chicago, Illinois

RENDERING SIZE
10" x 16" (25 cm x 41 cm)

MEDIUM
Freehand pen & ink,
color pencil, and pastel

PROJECT
Jacksonville Galleria

CLIENT
Anthony Belluschi Architects

RENDERING SIZE
12" x 16" (30 cm x 41 cm)

MEDIUM
Freehand felt tip pen and color pencil

700 SOUTH CLINTON STREET
CHICAGO, ILLINOIS 60607
312-987-0132
312-987-0099 FAX

PROJECT
600 North Michigan Avenue
Chicago, Illinois
CLIENT
Beyer Blinder Belle
RENDERING SIZE
16" x 23" (41 cm x 58 cm)
MEDIUM
Airbrush

PROJECT
600 North Michigan Avenue
Chicago, Illinois
CLIENT
Beyer Blinder Belle
RENDERING SIZE
22" x 33" (56 cm x 84 cm)
MEDIUM
Airbrush

James C. Smith

Trained in the fine arts of painting and printmaking at Northwestern University, James C. Smith was influenced by the work of the early-20th-century surrealist movement. Moods, expressions, and visual animation are basic creative elements of his illustrations. After graduating with a Master of Fine Arts degree, a seven-year interim career at a large architectural firm provided invaluable exposure to internationally renown projects designed by master architects. James teaches advanced illustration techniques at Harrington Institute in Chicago, where Smith enjoys both professional practice and teaching.

The Studio of James C. Smith provides expertise, service, and an unmatched work ethic. Depiction of the subject is affected by design criteria, project location, and intended uses of the illustrations. Compositions, media, color, and value are all carefully examined to formulate a basic creative strategy. Project budget is determined by three factors: complexity of the architecture, media, and schedule. Site visitation is extremely helpful to gain impressions and the character of the project area.

The Studio of James C. Smith provides complete illustration services. A typical commission defines media, schedule, and budget at the onset. James sketches ideas with the client to gain an understanding of the design and to form a genuine professional relationship. The Studio's computer system provides the mechanical means to plot designs, layouts, and graphics accurately. Typical commissions range from loose concept sketches through multiple airbrush presentation paintings.

PROJECT
600 North Michigan Avenue
Chicago, Illinois
CLIENT
Beyer Blinder Belle
RENDERING SIZE
22" x 33" (56 cm x 84 cm)
MEDIUM
Airbrush

PROJECT
The Rookery
Chicago, Illinois

CLIENT
Burnham and Root

RENDERING SIZE
32" x 24" (81 cm x 61 cm)

MEDIUM
Airbrush

PROJECT
The Rookery
Chicago, Illinois

CLIENT
Burnham and Root

RENDERING SIZE
32" x 24" (81 cm x 61 cm)

MEDIUM
Airbrush

PROJECT
The Rookery
Chicago, Illinois

CLIENT
Burnham and Root

RENDERING SIZE
10" x 30" (25 cm x 76 cm)

MEDIUM
Airbrush

PROJECT
The Rookery
Chicago, Illinois

CLIENT
Burnham and Root

RENDERING SIZE
20" x 15" (51 cm x 38 cm)

MEDIUM
Airbrush

PROJECT
The Rookery
Chicago, Illinois

CLIENT
Burnham and Root

RENDERING SIZE
32" x 24" (81 cm x 61 cm)

MEDIUM
Airbrush

PROJECT
77 West Wacker Drive
Chicago, Illinois

CLIENT
Ricardo Bofill

RENDERING SIZE
42" x 21" (107 cm x 53 cm)

MEDIUM
Airbrush

PROJECT
Henderson Square
Chicago, Illinois

CLIENT
Pappageorge & Haymes, Ltd.

RENDERING SIZE
29" x 35" (74 cm x 89 cm)

MEDIUM
Pencil and ink

PROJECT
The Cook County Dept. of
Corrections, Division 11,
Maximum Security Facility
Chicago, Illinois

CLIENT
Roula Associates, Chtd.

RENDERING SIZE
22" x 44" (56 cm x 112 cm)

MEDIUM
Airbrush

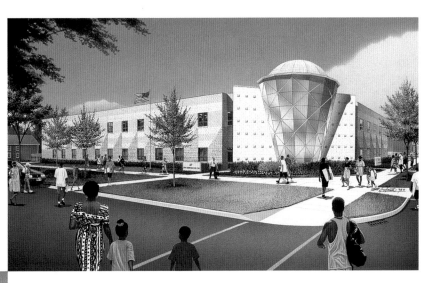

PROJECT
Railway Exchange Building
Chicago, Illinois

CLIENT
D. H. Burnham and Company

RENDERING SIZE
45" x 42" (114 cm x 107 cm)

MEDIUM
Airbrush

PROJECT
James Jordan Boys & Girls Club
Chicago, Illinois

CLIENT
Johnson & Lee, Ltd.

RENDERING SIZE
18" x 30" (46 cm x 76 cm)

MEDIUM
Airbrush

PROJECT
900 North Michigan
Avenue
Chicago, Illinois

CLIENT
Kohn Pedersen Fox

RENDERING SIZE
31" x 46" (79 cm x 117 cm)

MEDIUM
Airbrush

SUNS S.K. HUNG
445 FIFTH AVE, SUITE 19F.
NEW YORK, NEW YORK 10016
212-779-4977

Sun & Associates

CLIENT LIST

Emilio Ambasz & Associates
Edward Larrabee Barnes
John Burgee Architect with
Philip Johnson
The Eggers Group P.C.
Fox & Fowle Architects
Ulrich Franzen & Associates
Gruen Associates
Hardy Holzman Pfeiffer
Hellmuth Obata & Kassabaum
The Hillier Group
Kohn Pedersen Fox Associates
The Alan Lapidus Group
Murphy/Jahn Architect

Olympia & York Corp.
Pei, Cobb, Freed, & Partners
CesarPelli & Associates
RTKL Architects
Schuman Lichtenstein Clama
Efron Architects
Der Scutt Architect
Swanke Hayden Connell
Tishman Construction Co.
Weisberg Castro Associates

PROJECT
Messeturn Office Building
Frankfurt, Germany
ARCHITECT
Murphy/Jahn

PROJECT
Trinity Building
New York, New York
ARCHITECT
Swanke, Hayden, Connell

PROJECT
Museum of American Folk Art
New York, New York

ARCHITECT
Emilio Ambasz Associates

PROJECT
Longville Metropolitan
Center, Taiwan

ARCHITECT
C.Y. Lee

PROJECT
Hongkou Haborview Development, Taiwan

ARCHITECT
C.Y. Lee

PROJECT
The Corinthian
New York, New York

ARCHITECT
Der Scutt

PROJECT
New Office Building
Pittsburgh, Pennsylvania

ARCHITECT
RTKL

PROJECT
The Time Square
Development
New York, New York

ARCHITECT
Philip Johnson

PROJECT
The Rizzoli Building
New York, New York

ARCHITECT
Kohn, Pedersen, Fox
Associates

PROJECT
Kuanmei Hillside Residential Building, Taiwan

ARCHITECT
Chien Architect Associates

PROJECT
One Capital Holding Center
Louisville, Kentucky
ARCHITECT
John Burgee Architects with Philip Johnson

PROJECT
Trinity Building Lobby
New York, New York
ARCHITECT
Swanke, Hayden, Connell

PROJECT
City Center Complex
Taiwan
ARCHITECT
Artech Architects

PROJECT
City Towers Commercial Building
Taiwan

ARCHITECT
Artech Architects

PROJECT
Kern Corp., Brisbon, Australia

ARCHITECT
John Burgee Architects with
Philip Johnson

PROJECT
Proposed Casino Complex
Atlantic City, New Jersey

ARCHITECT
The Alan Lapidus Group

c/o NIETZ PRASCH SIGL UND PARTNER
ULMENSTRASSE 40 22299
HAMBURG GERMANY

PROJECT
Dresden Competition
Dresden, Germany
CLIENT
Nietz Prasch Sigl und Partner
RENDERING SIZE
5" x 10" (13 cm x 25 cm)
MEDIUM
Watercolor, pen, sepia ink

PROJECT
Rebuilding of Frauenkirche
Dresden, Germany
ARCHITECT OF COMPOSITION
Sergei E. Tchoban
RENDERING SIZE
24" x 18" (61 cm x 46 cm)
MEDIUM
Watercolor, pen, sepia ink

Sergei E. Tchoban

The most essential thing for architect and architectural illustrator Sergei E. Tchoban is the search for the most stimulating dialogue between the architectural composition, the architectural style, and the drawing technique implemented. The drawings presented in this book are executed in Tchoban's favorite medium—watercolor, pen, and sepia ink. This technique demonstrates the clarity of statement typical of modern architecture and, at the same time, provides enough scope to portray the various architectural details in a lively and artistic way. Tchoban's approach also allows him to create fantasy compositions and draft sketches for concrete projects without becoming naturalistic or using too many colors and materials.

PROJECT
Leipzig Terminal Competition
Leipzig, Germany
CLIENT
Nietz Prasch Sigl und Partner
RENDERING SIZE
14" x 14" (36 cm x 36 cm)
MEDIUM
Watercolor, pen, sepia ink

PROJECT
The Life on the Backside of the Town
(unbuilt)
ARCHITECT
Sergei E. Tchoban
RENDERING SIZE
24" x 24" (61 cm x 61 cm)
MEDIUM
Watercolor, pen, sepia ink

PROJECT
Market Place (unbuilt)
Rome, Italy
ARCHITECT OF COMPOSITION
Sergei E. Tchoban
RENDERING SIZE
14" x 25" (36 cm x 64 cm)
MEDIUM
Watercolor, pen, sepia ink

PROJECT
Architecture and Sculpture (unbuilt)
ARCHITECT OF COMPOSITION
Sergei E. Tchoban
RENDERING SIZE
20" x 20" (51 cm x 51 cm)
MEDIUM
Watercolor, pen, sepia ink

PROJECT
Two Lives (unbuilt)
RENDERING SIZE
24" x 18" (61 cm x 46 cm)
MEDIUM
Watercolor, pen, sepia ink

PROJECT
The Road into the Church
Prague, Czechoslovakia
ARCHITECT OF COMPOSITION
Sergei E. Tchoban
RENDERING SIZE
17" x 12" (43 cm x 31 cm)
MEDIUM
Watercolor, pen, sepia ink

PROJECT
Monument
ARCHITECT
Sergei E. Tchoban
RENDERING SIZE
14" x 14" (36 cm x 36 cm)
MEDIUM
Watercolor, pen, sepia ink

PARTNER LIST

nps and partner, Architects BDA, Hamburg, Berlin, Dresden
W. Nietz, A. Prasch, P. Sigl, S. Tchoban, E. Voss

4141 Lybyer Avenue
Miami, Florida 33133
305-663-8347
305-663-2575 fax

PROJECT
South Pointe Development
Miami Beach, Florida

Curtis James Woodhouse

Curtis Woodhouse is a Miami-based architect and illustrator who feels that his design and planning experience is essential when working with clients and producing successful illustration. While favoring watercolor, Woodhouse works with a variety of media at several scales and degrees of refinement. Much of Woodhouse's work involves direct design collaboration, and he has participated in many charrettes and on-site workshops.

PROJECT
Riverboat Casino Proposal
Saint Louis, Missouri

CLIENT
Ellerbee Becket

PROJECT
Miami International
Airport, Concourse H

CLIENT
Perez and Perez

PROJECT
Sasson Hotel Tower
Miami Beach, Florida
CLIENT
Schapiro Associates

225

PROJECT
Meadowbrook Housing
Montreal, Quebec, Canada

CLIENT
Schapiro Associates

PROJECT
Berlinerstrasse Housing
Potsdam, Germany

CLIENT
Moore, Ruble, Yudell

PROJECT
Official All Star Cafe, Times Square
New York, New York

CLIENT
Rockwell Architecture

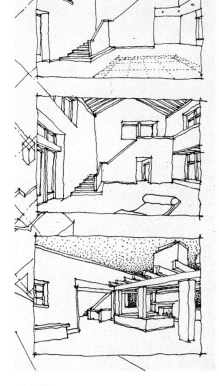

PROJECT
Design Studies, Playa Vista Housing
Los Angeles, California

CLIENT
Moore, Ruble, Yudell

PROJECT
Ocean Forest
Sea Island, Georgia

CLIENT
Architectural Design Group

PROJECT
H.H.I. Automobile Showroom
Fort Lauderdale, Florida

CLIENT
Bermello Ajamil & Partners Inc.

PROJECT
South Pointe Development
Miami Beach, Florida

228   *Curtis James Woodhouse*

PROJECT
South Pointe Charrette
Miami Beach, Florida

CLIENT
Arquitectonica with STA

PROJECT
Bobo
Marathon Key, Florida

MEDIUM
Watercolor

PROJECT
Study Sketch
San Francisco, California

MEDIUM
Colored pencil

PROJECT
Playa Vista Office Campus
Los Angeles, California

CLIENT
Moore, Ruble, Yudell

Curtis James Woodhouse   229

DELINEATION GRAPHIX
238 BULWARA ROAD, ULTIMO
SYDNEY, NSW 2007, AUSTRALIA

PROJECT
Urban Renewal of
O'Connell Street
Dublin, Ireland

ARCHITECT
Keane Murphy & Duff

MEDIUM
Tempera, watercolor,
airbrush effects

Serge Zaleski, ARAIA, FSAI, AAAI, ASAP

PROJECT
Pandaland Proposed Theme Park
Shanghai, People's Republic of China

CLIENT
Pandaland Party Ltd.

DESIGNER
Attractions International
Belt Collins

MEDIUM
Tempera, watercolor, airbrush effects

PROJECT
Exhibition Center/Aerial Overview
Brisbane, Queensland, Australia

ARCHITECT
John Andrews International

MEDIUM
Tempera, watercolor, airbrush effects

ASAP Award for Excellence, 1995.
Included in Architecture in
Perspective catalogue and
exhibition, 1995, Seattle, WA.

PROJECT
Humpy Music CD cover for
the Gondwanaland Band

MEDIUM
Tempera, watercolor,
airbrush effects

Included in ASAP Architecture
in Perspective 11 exhibition,
1996, Boston, MA.

PROJECT
Sega World Virtual Reality
Amusement Park/Interior
Darling Harbor, Sydney,
NSW, Australia

CLIENT
Sega-Ozisoft Party Ltd.

ARCHITECT
Cameron Chisholm Nicol
Australia

MEDIUM
Tempera, watercolor,
airbrush effects

PROJECT
Safari Resort, Nairobi, Kenya

CLIENT
Paradise Investments
Korea

DESIGNER
Belt Collins
Australia

MEDIUM
Tempera, watercolor,
airbrush effects

PROJECT
Extensions to the Port of Newcastle
NSW, Australia

ARCHITECT
Port Authority, Newcastle

MEDIUM
Tempera, watercolor, airbrush effects

PROJECT
Proposed Refurbishment of Princes Pier
Auckland, New Zealand

ARCHITECT
Manning Mitchell Architects
New Zealand

MEDIUM
Tempera, watercolor, airbrush effects

PROJECT
Exhibition Centre
Melbourne, Victoria, Australia

ARCHITECT
Denton Corker Marshall

MEDIUM
Tempera, watercolor, airbrush effects

PROJECT
Exhibition Center/Rear Plaza
Brisbane, Queensland, Australia

ARCHITECT
John Andrews International

MEDIUM
Tempera, watercolor, airbrush effects

PROJECT
Backtown Railway Station
Sydney, NSW, Australia

ARCHITECT
State Rail NSW

MEDIUM
Tempera, watercolor, airbrush effects

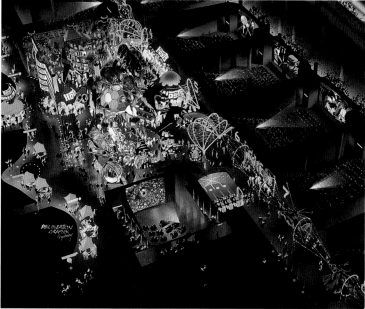

PROJECT
Multiple cinema entry prototype

MEDIUM
Tempera and watercolor on
Bainbridge board

Winner, Architecture in
Perspective 11 Juror's award

PROJECT
CBD 1 Tower
Proposed Offices
Sydney, NSW, Australia

CLIENT
Kumagai Gumi Party Ltd.

ARCHITECT
Stephenson & Turner
International

MEDIUM
Tempera, watercolor,
airbrush effects

PROJECT
Refurbishment of the Finger Wharves
Sydney, NSW, Australia

ARCHITECT
Denton Corker Marshall

MEDIUM
Tempera, watercolor, airbrush effects

Serge Zaleski   **235**

Bibliography

Published Sources of Information on Professional Rendering and Renderers

1. American Society of Architectural Illustrators, *Architecture in Perspective.* New York: VNR, 1992.

2. American Society of Architectural Illustrators, *Architecture in Perspective.*
[Nos. 1–7]————, Boston: ASAP, 1986–1992.
[Nos. 8, 9]————, San Francisco: Pomegranate Artbooks, 1993, 1994.
[Nos. 10, 11]————, Rockport MA: Rockport Publishers, 1995, 1996.

3. Burden, Ernest Ii, *Architectural Delineation— A Photographic Approach to Presentation.* New York: McGraw-Hill, 1971.

4. Chen, John, *Architecture in Pen and Ink.* New York: McGraw-Hill, 1995.

5. Crowe, Philip, *Architectural Rendering.* Mies, Switzerland: Rotovision, 1991.

6. Grice, Gordon, ed. *The Art of Architectural Illustration.* Natick, MA: Resource World Inc.; Rockport, MA: Rockport Publishers, 1993.

7. Gupthill, Arthur L., *Rendering in Pen and Ink.* New York: Watson Gupthill, 1976.

8. ————. *Rendering in Pencil.* New York: Watson Gupthill, 1977.

9. Jacoby, Helmut, *New Techniques of Architectural Rendering, 2nd Ed.* New York: VNR, 1981.

10. Japanese Association of Architectural Renderers, *Perspective, 1990.* Tokyo: JARA, 1990.

11. Korean Architectural Perspectivists, *Architectural Perspective.* Seoul, Korea: KAPA, 1995.

12. Lacy, Bill, 100 *Contemporary Architects— Drawings & Sketches.* New York: Abrams, 1991.

13. Leich, Jean Ferriss, *Architectural Visions— The Drawings of Hugh Ferriss.* New York: Whitney Library of Design, 1980.

14. Luscombe, Desley, & Anne Peden, *Picturing Architecture.* Tortola, BVI: Craftsman House, 1992.

15. McGarry, Richard and Greg Madsen, *Marker Magic.* New York: VNR, 1993.

16. Nevins, Deborah & Robert A. M. Stern, *The Architect's Eye—American Architectural Drawing from 1799–1978.* New York: Pantheon, 1979.

17. New York Society of Renderers, *Architectural & Interior Rendering, 1992 Portfolio.* New York: NYSR, 1992.

18. Oles, Paul Stevenson, *Architectural Illustration: The Value Delineation Process.* New York: VNR, 1979.

19. ———. *Drawing the Future.* New York: VNR, 1988.

20. Papadakis, Dr. Andreas, ed., *Drawing into Architecture, an Architectural Design Profile.* New York, London: Academy Editions, St. Martin's Press, 1989.

21. Resource World, Inc., *Architectural Design Collaborators.* Natick, MA: Resource World, Inc. [Nos. 1, 2, & 3]———. 1990, 1991, 1992.

22. Porter, Tom, *Architectural Drawing.* New York: VNR, Hamlyn Publishing /Amazon Publishing, 1990.

23. ———. *Architectural Drawing Masterclass.* Charles. New York: Charles Scribner's Sons, 1993.

24. Rochon, Richard & Harold Linton, *Color in Architectural Illustration.* New York: VNR, 1989.

25. Schaller, Thomas W., *Architecture in Watercolour.* New York: VNR, 1990.

26. Society of Architectural & Industrial Illustrators, *The SAI Directory.* Stroud, Glos., UK: SAI, 1992.

27. Stamp, Gavin, *The Great Perspectivists.* New York: Rizzoli, 1982.

28. Walker, Derek, *Helmut Jacoby—Architectural Drawings, 1968–1976.* New York: Architectural Book Publishing Co., 1977.

29. Wilson, Peter, *Contemporary British Architectural Drawing.* Berlin: Academy Editions, 1993.

30. Woods, Lebbeus, *Lebbeus Woods: Anarchitecture.* New York, London: Academy Editions, St. Martin's Press, 1992.

Directory

Sachiko Asai
AZ Project Inc.
563 Ishiyama, Minamiku
Sapporo 005 Japan
011-591-1683
011-591-9519 fax

Richard C. Baehr
305 Northern Boulevard
Great Neck, New York 11021
516-466-0470

Anita S. Bice
Commercial Artistry
1009 Park Avenue
Moody, Alabama 35004

Frank M. Costantino
13-B Pauline Street
Winthrop, MA 02152
617-846-4766

Angelo DeCastro
Rua do Alto da Milha, 50A
São João do Estoril, 2765
Portugal
+351-1-467-1010/466-0624
+351-1-466-1648 fax

Lee Dunnette
430 East 20th Street, 5B
New York, New York 10009
212-260-4240

Bill Evans
714 First Avenue West
Seattle, Washington 98119
206 282-8785
206 282-8764 fax

Al Forster
PO Box 326
The Sea Ranch, California 95497
707-785-2184
800-233-0658
707-785-2264 Fax

Gilbert Gorski
Gorski & Associates P.C.
6633 Spokane Avenue
Lincolnwood, Illinois 60646
847-329-1340

Jane Grealy
Jane Grealy and Associates
Suite 7, 322 Old Cleveland Road
Coorparoo, Brisbane, Qld 4151
Australia
+61-7-3394-4333
+61-7-3849-0646 fax

Gordon Grice
Gordon Grice & Associates
35 Church Street #205
Toronto, Ontario
Canada M5E 1T3
416-536-9191
416-696-8866 fax

Andy Hickes
Digital Architectural Illustration
205 Third Avenue
New York, New York 10003
212-677-8054

Willem van den Hoed
1000 Huizen
Lange Geer 44, 2611 PW Delft
The Netherlands
31.15.2133382
31.15.2120448 fax

Douglas E. Jamieson
827 ½ Via de la Paz
Pacific Palisades, California
310 573-1155
310 459-1429

Takuji Kariya
RIYA Co. Ltd.
1-5-5 406 Tomobuchi Cho
Miyakojimaku
Osaka 534 Japan
06 924 3637

Ronald J. Love
3891 Bayridge Avenue
West Vancouver
British Columbia
Canada V7V 3J3
604-922-3033
604-922-2393 fax

Bruce MacDonald
217 Pine St., Suite 1200
Seattle WA 98101
Seattle 206-621-8936
Portland 503-292-2100

Charlie Manus
Architectural Presentation Arts
43 Union Avenue #1
Memphis, Tennessee 38103

Michael McCann
Michael McCann Associates Ltd.
2 Gibson Avenue
Toronto, Ontario
Canada M5R 1T5

Robert McIlhargey/Lori Brown
McIlhargey Brown & Associates
Design Consultants & Illustration
Suite 410
1639 West Second Avenue
Vancouver, British Columbia
Canada V6J-1H3
604-736-7897
604-736-9763 fax

Morello Design Studio, GMBH
Kiningergasse 4
1120 Vienna
Austria, Europe
(0222) 804-43-57
c/o James Cavello
578 West Broadway
New York, NY 10012
212-925-5700

Paul Stevenson Oles
FAIA/Advanced Media Design Inc.
One Gateway Center
Newton, Massachusetts 02158
617-527-6790/800-697-4720
617-527-6790 fax
401-272-6240 fax
soles@mit.edu

Stephen Parker
802 Kipling Way
Weldon Springs, Missouri 63304
314-441-8370

Eugene Radvenis
E. V. Radvenis Inc.
410-1639 West 2nd Avenue
Vancouver, British Colombia
Canada V6J 1H3
604-736-5430
604-736-9763 fax

Barbara Worth Ratner
Architectural Illustration
828 Charles Allen Drive, N.E.
Atlanta, Georgia 30308
404-876-3943
404-876-3943 fax

Michael Reardon
5433 Boyd Avenue
Oakland, California 94618
510-655-7030 phone and fax

Richard Rochon
Rochon Associates, Inc.
13530 Michigan Avenue
Suite 205
Dearborn, Michigan 48126
313-584-9580
313-584-4071 fax

Thomas W. Schaller
2112 Broadway #407
New York, New York 10023
212-362-5524
212-364-5719 fax

Hideo Shirai
Shirai Pers House
31-8-213 Honcho,
Wako-shi, Saitama-ken
351-01 Japan
048-465-1615 phone and fax

Rael D. Slutsky
Rael D. Slutsky & Associates, Inc.
Architectural Imaging
351 Milford Road
Deerfield, Illinois 60015

James C. Smith
700 South Clinton Street
Chicago, Illinois 60607
312-987-0132
312-987-0099 fax

Sun & Associates
Suns S.K. Hung
445 Fifth Ave, Suite 19F
New York, New York 10016
212-779-4977

Sergei E. Tchoban
c/o Nietz Prasch Sigl und Partner
Ulmenstrasse 40 22299
Hamburg Germany

Curtis James Woodhouse
4141 Lybyer Avenue
Miami, Florida 33133
305-663-8347
305-663-2575 fax

Serge Zaleski
Delineation Graphix
238 Bulwara Road, Ultimo
Sydney, NSW 2007, Australia